SUPER

KELVIN DAVIS

– a celebration

Compiled by BARRY WEBB

First published in the United Kingdom in 2016 by
SKD Publications, 45 Old Meadows Walk, West Harnham,
Salisbury, Wiltshire, SP2 8PA

British Library Cataloguing in Publication Data

A catalogue record for this book is available from the British Library

ISBN 978-1-5262-0154-6

Typeset in Myriad Pro 12 point

Designed and printed in Great Britain by Salisbury Printing Company Limited, Salisbury, Wiltshire

Contents

Davis, K. G.

Surname	DAVIS
First Names	KELVIN GEOFFREY
Date of birth	29 September 1976
Place of Birth	Bedford, England
Parents	Geoffrey and Lilian
Sisters	Marcia and Faye
Wife	Kelly (née Greening)
Date of marriage	9 June 2001
Place of marriage	All Saints Church, Leighton Buzzard
Children	Emelia, Sonnie and Buddy
Occupation	Goalkeeper
Main Achievement	301 appearances for Southampton Football Club

Foreword

by Steve Root

'Rooty' is one of Kelvin's oldest and closest friends

When I was approached to write the foreword to this book I was totally overwhelmed. There will no doubt be well-known people, players, managers, Saints players, past and present, quoted within these pages and elsewhere, not to mention the family that Kelvin treasures so dearly. So, when I was asked to share my thoughts about him and his time at this great club it surprised me, but filled me with huge pride.

I am neither famous nor wealthy and as much as I have tried (and believe me, I have tried) I have never played football at anything other than a low level, such as in Sunday leagues. However, following Kelvin's career has given me a rare insight into the life of professional football and the dedication it takes to succeed in this sport, let alone becoming club captain at one of England's finest family football clubs.

I have had the honour of being his oldest friend and his best man, as well as godfather to his three beautiful children. We have had some brilliant laughs in the past, most of which you cannot put in a book for families but I shall share a couple of stories.

First, though, I have no hesitation whatsoever in sharing with you that when it comes to Kelvin, the saying *"show me the boy and I will show you the man"* really does apply.

The first time I met Kelv he had long hair to his shoulders and he was playing local football, although he probably did just as much Motocross with his dad Geoff. When he played football for Corinthians in Leighton Buzzard and then for Stony Stratford Youth he played in midfield. This suited me fine because, unfortunately for me, I was, and still am a goalkeeper.

He first committed himself to the number 1 position in our first trial at Vandyke upper school. Many were the times that we used to get to the changing room and see *"number 1, Kelvin Davis"* written on the wall. Our school friends will remember the games in which our PE teacher Sean Downey would *"release Kelvin"* to play in the outfield and bring me on as a substitute in goal. When I spoke to our former teacher recently he immediately recalled a semi-final in which we needed a goal and sure enough Kelvin came out and put away a header that only he could have scored. One-on-one with the goalkeeper Kelvin nodded it in, taking a full punch in the face in the process.

He always had a real confidence about him and in school this could sometimes be misconstrued as arrogance and land him in a few scrapes, nearly always with the older lads. The important thing about Kelvin is that he was brought up by his parents to know right from wrong. As a result, he would always stand up for what he believed was right and he would see it through. Although this went on to serve him really well in his professional career, at school it meant that there was the occasional punch up but Kelvin won more than he lost.

A lot of people think they are winners but they do not actually know how to get there. Kelvin did know and he prepared meticulously, analysing his performance after each game. Early signs of his fierce competitiveness emerged when we were at school. In the summer we all tried to get straight out of lessons when the lunch bell went so as to get a tennis court. Kelvin would be there in a shot waiting for the first serve.

The girls were not so bothered about tennis and would run across the court, taking the balls and generally trying to get his attention. Being about four stone overweight I never had such distractions and used to find it pretty amusing, as did Kelvin – most of the time. However, I do remember one lunchtime where we were playing and one of the girls, Hayley, kept running on, nicking the ball and then lobbing it down the playground. I could see Kelvin getting more and more annoyed and he said to me, *"Rooty, if she comes on once more I am going to unleash the big forehand".* Sure enough about a minute later she ran on laughing and goading us and as she passed him *wallop* – he gave her the full Boris Becker on her backside and off she went straight to the head of year. I was there to hear Kelvin explain that he had not hit her that hard. She was then asked to lift her skirt (it was the 90's so that was not seen as a weird request). She did so and revealed a perfect crisscross pattern on her left cheek. Kelvin immediately started sniggering and, if the truth be told, the head of year was trying not to laugh too. That is one of the things with Kelvin, he could get away with such behaviour because he has always known how to make people laugh.

One trait he would take into adult life was doing anything that would raise a laugh and possibly shock people, although I think there are only so many times you can get your willy out as a grown man and not get arrested for it. The first time my wife and I went on holiday with Kelvin and Kelly, he decided to ride a two year-old's tricycle with squeaky wheels around the pool – fully naked – not once but twice.

The ruthless nature of Kelvin's sense of humour came through once when we were about 17 and on holiday with other YTS trainees who were all typically fit and bronzed. I confided in him that I was really nervous about taking my t-shirt off as I was about 19 stone and I did not want anyone laughing at me and embarrassing me in front of the sunbathers round the pool. Kelvin looked me in the eye and said with the utmost sincerity, *"Mate, don't worry about it, I've got your back and we will style it out together. If any of the lads get on your case, I will sort them out".*

So, buoyed by his vote of confidence and support, I plucked up the courage to climb silently into the pool and slip off my t-shirt and place it on the side. I must have been in the pool for about two hours, all the time keeping my shoulders under the water. Eventually I decided to get out on the quiet side of the crowded pool, thinking that my excursion had been a total success. But how wrong could I be? I got one leg on the side of the pool to hear Mr Davis bellowing, *"Quick! Quick! It's getting out! Harpoon it, Harpoon it!"* There was rapturous laughter all the way round the pool because my 'friend' had waited for two hours, telling everyone to make the loudest possible fuss and to direct all attention my way.

At the time I thought, *"Cheers mate"* but looking back I realise it was just his way of saying, *"There's no need to worry about stuff like that".*

Kelvin was popular without really trying to be and he always sees other people for who they are. You could be a fat, spotty 17 year-old or Ronaldo and Kelv would treat you the same. He has always been so grounded and has never forgotten where he came from.

From house parties to VIP invitations at top London clubs our friendship has not changed. He takes the mickey and I do what I can to stitch him up when I have had a drink or two. Over the years he has slapped me, hit me with a bamboo cane (while I was asleep and naked), cut out the pockets of my best clothes that I bought especially for a night out and smacked me round the face with a lady's sandal – and more. All of which I can honestly say I have deserved.

Over the years I have managed to get him back and one particular incident was in Spain about 12 years ago. He was playing for either Ipswich or Sunderland at the time and it was an international break and players who were not on international duty got a couple of days off. We went to a club and got a posh table, one where you get a stupidly expensive bottle of spirit and then spend all night attempting to drink it. Well, in my world when you pay that much you drink it.

As the evening drew on the effects of a litre of vodka were taking their toll and to get Kelvin's attention I decided a quick game of 'ice darts' was required. The game is simple: you get an ice cube from the bucket, lob it up in the air aiming to land it in your mate's glass and splash their drink all over them. Anyway, my 'darts' were way off target and I very gently (honestly, it was not that hard) managed to flick the ice cube straight into Kelvin's eye. The table went silent and Kelvin started to get redder and redder and then a tear of blood started to trickle down his face. He grabbed me but after my speedy explanation we were laughing about it within five minutes.

However, the next day the makings of a proper shiner were showing and, by the time he played for the Saints in a live televised game against Watford, his black eye was so visible that the commentator said during the game, *"If you are wondering about Kelvin Davis's black eye, it has not happened in the game. Apparently his mate threw an ice cube at him – that's his story and he is sticking to it".* I was at home laughing my head off.

I could go on for a long time telling stories about my best mate, but let me try and sum him up. He is the most loyal friend in my life and his loyalty has shown in his football career too. He is not a money grabber and certainly does not seek out the bright lights. He is trustworthy and honest even if that means sharing harsh truths with people. He is the type of person that people want to be like.

He has a crazy sense of humour but anyone who has ever played in a team will tell you that banter is vital for morale and he has bundles of it. Kelvin was always going to make something of himself because he has that secret ingredient, charisma. Whether it is as a footballer, a motocross champion, a top earner in business or whatever, people like him succeed, pure and simple.

His time with Southampton has been like a dream and he loves the club passionately, even with the hard times alongside the many good times. I am ready to admit that watching him make his 300th appearance for the Saints, next to my wife and son and a number of his family was the most emotional moment I have had in football. To think that the mate I warmed up with as a kid was at the Etihad stadium 25 years later facing shots from the likes of Frank Lampard and Sergio Agüero is hard to put into words. The simple reason is that it means so much to Kelvin to represent the club.

I hope this gives an insight into Kelvin from an old mate's perspective. It is my privilege to have the opportunity to say that, for all the achievements in his career, especially during the last ten years with the Saints, the person I will always see is Kelv, just Kelv. He is my best mate, I love him and wish him all the success and rewards that come his way in life, he deserves them.

God bless mate,
Rooty.

Preface

It was both a privilege and an honour for me to be asked to compile a book to celebrate **Kelvin Davis** – or **Super Kelvin Davis, SKD** or **Super Kel** as he is known to fans and to colleagues and staff at Southampton Football Club. Coming at a time when he completes his tenth season at the club the book also reflects on a loyal footballer and a proud family man.

This is not a full biography in the conventional sense but in seeking to paint a picture of a significant part of his life it also looks at the influences on Kelvin and those things that shaped him before he became a Saint.

Saints supporters know only too well what an extraordinary period this has been in the history of our football club. The book covers both the highs and lows of an eventful ten seasons with Kelvin recalling special moments on and off the pitch, his relationship with team mates and others, his roles as both team and club captain and how his family and friends have been a constant source of support and an influence on him. Most important he also reflects on his reasons for staying at the club.

While compiling the book I have discovered that Kelvin is not only a highly professional footballer: he is a strong family man, a clown and practical joker but someone who is always sensitive to the feelings of others. He is a man who is highly respectful of people inside and outside football and this is reflected in the fact that he does not want to use the book as an opportunity to *"have a pop"* as he calls it. He simply wants to take the opportunity to reflect honestly and openly on his feelings at significant times in his ten seasons.

Saints fans will relate to some, if not all of the memories in the book, especially those that they have witnessed for themselves. The accounts given are intentionally serious and amusing, reflecting the man himself.

I am very grateful to the many people who have contributed to this celebration account but a particular debt of gratitude goes to Kelly Davis both for her contributions to the book and for her stalwart support for Kelvin during his time at Southampton and before.

Barry Webb
April 2016

Friday 21 July: Arrived at Southampton

If you think this sounds like the start of a tedious travel diary you would be wrong. The past ten seasons at Southampton Football Club have not been tedious – far from it. Eventful – tense, exciting, uplifting, disheartening – all those things but definitely eventful, and one man has been a constant through it all.

Kelvin Davis signed for the Saints on Friday 21 July 2006, just two months before his 30th birthday and approaching the start of the Saints' second season in the Championship.

He recalls with affection the day when he came south to sign from Sunderland. People who believe in premonitions and the like might have read something into the fact that Kelvin and Kelly Davis got married in All Saints church. Although this is just an amusing coincidence it is curiously true that Kelvin had felt a hankering to play for the Saints three months earlier. In April 2006, just 13 weeks before he would sign for the Saints, Kelvin came south on a trip in the Premier League with Sunderland to play Portsmouth. The Sunderland squad flew down to Southampton from where they would make the journey to Portsmouth by coach.

The flight path into Southampton airport took them over St Mary's Stadium and as Kelvin recalls, *"I remember flying down from a drab afternoon in Sunderland to a sunny day. I had a window seat which I always tried to get and flying over the top of the stadium I can remember looking down on the sun thinking 'I'd love to play there'".* But there had been more serious considerations when Kelvin made the move to Southampton.

He is very honest about the fact that he didn't have the best time in his career at Sunderland. It was a strain on the family and his wife, Kelly, in particular could not settle in the area. He freely admits that in that sort of situation you need to make more of an effort and, indeed, Kelvin and Kelly did make an effort to make it work. They felt however that the football club was not able to offer them much support in their efforts to settle. The club was not necessarily unique in that respect. Despite being a Premier League club they needed to operate within a tight budget and, as Kelvin observes, *"Things cost money – I can understand that. But it got to the stage where you felt that if an opportunity came up I would need to press on for the better of myself and the family".*

So, having become open to the idea of looking for another club Kelvin shared his feelings with his advisor and representative who has helped him for nearly his whole career saying that *"it's affecting my private life and my family life and it's not really how I want to live".* A close bond has developed between them and as Kelvin puts it, *"I knew him well and he obviously knew me very well".*

One thing about Kelvin is that, as well as being honest and open, he is an honourable person. He respected the fact that he had been happy to sign a contract and he was content to take the wages and, therefore, it was in his nature to behave in a professional and honourable manner. If nothing had come up, then it is clear that Kelvin would have honoured his contract at Sunderland.

Kelvin spoke to the powers that be at Sunderland and made it known he would like to be made aware of any calls or interest in him, whether at the end of the season or during the close season. He quietly and politely made it clear to the club that he would like to consider any options. If something seemed right for him and his family, and right for the club, then he would like to look to move on. He sensed that he was not going to upset the club unduly because they had been relegated to the Championship and would undoubtedly be seeking ways both to reduce their wages bill and to bring in some money to the club.

So, when the opportunity to move to Southampton came about it was an easy decision to make. Kelvin was on a week-long pre-season training trip in Bath. He describes the timing of the chance to go to Southampton as *"quite strange".* It was at a time when the Sunderland players found themselves *"all in the same boat",* having been relegated and with no manager. They were doing their best to stick together in their shared circumstances. For Kelvin it was probably the best time that he'd spent with the group but here he was actively trying to leave the club. As Kelvin says now, *"I remember that week down in Bath was the first time I felt a connection amongst the lads there".*

His advisor rang him to say that an agreement had been reached between Southampton and Sunderland despite an issue with the fee but this had been resolved by agreeing an initial transfer fee of £1 million with further payments based on appearances. Sunderland had tried very hard to keep hold of Kelvin but as he says *"his mind was made up".*

With heavy understatement Kelvin recalls the *"nice feeling"* he had when he phoned his wife Kelly who was still in Sunderland. The conversation essentially boiled down to, *"pack your bags, grab the kids and get on the motorway".* Kelly recalls how she *"packed three suitcases and two kids and never looked back".* She also confesses that she never went back to the house in Stockton-on-Tees and that there was probably still coffee in the coffee pot. Fortunately, the percolator was turned off. Eventually it was one of Kelvin's sisters and her husband who went north and cleared the house for them.

As Kelvin reflects, *"as a footballer it's the nature of the job that one day you're training here and the next day you're training there."* Now it was the *"next day"* as he arrived at Southampton for the start of a long relationship with the club.

It would be pleasing to suppose that Kelvin jumped at the chance to come to Southampton because he wanted to join a club that looked after people. But he knew too little about the club to make such a judgement at the time. He is very honest and says, without any harshness, that this was not the primary consideration that attracted him to our club. His interest in Southampton was heightened in view of the fact that George Burley had become the Saints' manager and Malcolm Webster had joined him as goalkeeping coach.

Kelvin had a long-standing and very strong relationship with Malcolm who had been his mentor at Ipswich Town and before that, aged only 19, Kelvin used to have two afternoon training sessions a week with Malcolm at Luton Town.

Malcolm had left Ipswich to follow George Burley but such was the bond and friendship between coach and goalkeeper that Malcolm actually took time to explain in person to Kelvin that it was an opportunity not to be missed to go and work with George. Subsequently, the season later Kelvin moved to Sunderland and then George and Malcolm both came to Southampton. Kelvin had the feeling *"almost instantly"* that Southampton was going to be his next club.

With both Malcolm Webster and Kevin Miller at the club Kelvin did not delay to come down and sign the contract. He recalls staying in Winchester that evening and then it was *"all systems go"*. He goes on to say, *"It was great to get there"*, and after all these years he even remembers that his first lunch was at Banana Wharf by the marina in Southampton.

The notion that Southampton was a *"family club"* became clear from the people Kelvin met on the day he signed. *"The way that I was treated I felt special. I felt like they wanted me"*.

He speaks affectionately about the people who made him feel so welcome and who were there to help out in any way they could. In particular Kelvin recalls the warmth shown to him by Barry Fox who, at that time, was training ground manager as well as almost fulfilling the role of 'player liaison'.

And so Kelvin's stay at Southampton Football Club began and it would go on to last for at least ten seasons. Administration might have conspired to make him leave but he has remained and as club captain his influence has been massive.

The foundations for the way in which he has conducted himself throughout his career were undoubtedly laid at his former clubs before he became a Saint. At his first club, Luton Town, he particularly developed as a goalkeeper, as a professional footballer and as a person.

Life Before the Saints

Prior to joining the Saints Kelvin had played 386 games for six clubs, including games as a trainee at Luton Town:

	Luton Town	105
	Wimbledon	146
	Ipswich Town	93
	Sunderland	35
Loans:	*Torquay United*	*4*
	Hartlepool United	*3*

In his formative years at Luton Town Kelvin learned a great deal from Malcolm Webster who was to become his long-standing coach, mentor and close friend. Kelvin also learned two lessons from the then Luton Town manager David Pleat. The first of these, when he was just 14, is his experience of *"knowing who people are"* – a story that his father Geoff still relishes.

After a week's trial with the Luton under-14s Kelvin was asked if he wanted to play a game for them. He could hardly refuse especially as the scheduled game was against Brentford who just happened to be the club Geoff Davis had supported man and boy. It was a high-scoring game, as is often the case with youth football. The collective memories of the Davis family are not entirely reliable, suggesting that it was 6-4, 5-4 or 4-3. However, Geoff Davis is adamant that it was 5-3 in favour of Luton and, after all, he should know as it was his club, Brentford, who lost.

25 years later Kelvin remembers having a *"very mixed game"* in that he made a number of saves but also conceded several goals. One goal came about when the ball bounced near the edge of the box, the opposing player got in front of him and the ball ended up in the back of the net. When half-time or full-time came (memories are inconsistent on this) the players walked off and made a little circle with the coach.

Kelvin takes up the story, *"This guy approached me and started chatting about one of the goals, talking about my starting position and, if I could start more advanced, behind the back four as it was then, there would be a chance to make more saves and in particular stop that goal. I remember listening to him and accepting what he had to say".*

When Kelvin walked off the pitch he was immediately approached by his team mate Paul McClaren ('Macca'). He had only met Macca during the week but he would go on to become one of Kelvin's closest friends and join Rooty as one of his two best men at his wedding.

Macca said, *"You know who that was?"*

"No idea. Ain't got a clue mate".

"That's David Pleat, the manager".

"Oh right".

Kelvin was so focused that he was not always aware of who was around him and admits that it says a lot about him how he is even now. *"I probably don't know too many other people and who I meet".* But he goes on to praise David Pleat who took the time not only to watch a youth team game but also to give advice to a young prospect. Kelvin's parents have since met David Pleat at Saints matches and he always displays huge respect for Kelvin and on one occasion went on to tell them that he realised, *"how important they have been to Kelvin and how supportive they've been through all that he has done".*

Kelvin has also kept in contact with David Pleat, including when he wrote to Kelvin about a player who was being released. It seemed that David Pleat was trying to see if there was a position at Kelvin's club for him. As Kelvin says, *"It shows his character. In football you can help people in different ways and he's still trying to support a player".*

The second lesson also involved David Pleat when Kelvin tried to negotiate his first contract. In essence he was not very knowledgeable in the business side of football, something which he feels he cannot be accused of these days.

When he was 17, 18, and 19 Kelvin was getting phone calls from different agents but from his perspective there was a wall growing between clubs and agents. Kelvin knew that some clubs held a view that agents were going to *"ruin the game"*. He decided to negotiate with David Pleat himself but his very first contract negotiation gave him *"a fantastic lesson about football"*. Although Kelvin uses the word *"negotiate"* he says that it seemed more like, *"he told me where to sign"*. But Kelvin Davis had always been, in his own words, *"quite confident"* and he felt that as a goalkeeper he deserved special consideration.

Kelvin was called into the office of Mr Pleat who said, *"There's a two-year professional contract I want you to sign. It's a standard first contract that everyone gets. You get the privilege to sign the contract. It's the same contract that Paul's got"*. Paul was Paul McClaren who Kelvin shared a house with at the time.

Kelvin recalls thinking to himself, *"Well, hold on a minute, I'm a goalkeeper, Paul's a midfielder and if he gets on the bench he's going to have a lot more opportunities to play than I am. So, I'm going to see if I can change something in this contract"*.

There was no time for Kelvin to read it. The contract was there and so was the pen. Kelvin politely thanked Mr Pleat but he went on to express the view that if he got on the bench he should at least get half of his appearance money. He knew that to get on the bench would be a massive achievement but he faced a lot more hurdles to get over before he played. Kelvin also chose to mention his team mate Paul, pointing out that his opportunities were going to be far greater than Kelvin's in terms of the percentage time spent playing as opposed to sitting on the bench.

Mr Pleat said, *"So what are you saying?"*

"Well, if I get on the bench I'd like half of my appearance money".

"Are you sure?"

"Yes".

"Okay we can do that", said the manager and that was it.

A couple of days later Kelvin proudly declared to one of the more experienced pros, *"I think I've done quite well actually. I've negotiated that I'll get 50% of my appearance money if I make it on a bench".*

Open-mouthed, his team mate replied, *"You effin' idiot. You get all your appearance money if you're on the bench anyway!"*

It was an important lesson for a 17 year-old and he started to think that he would need some form of representation. But he did nothing about it immediately.

....

Luton had promising young 'keepers and Kelvin recalls three who he played alongside in his early career. Nathan Abbey is now joint manager with his brother Zema at Arsley Town in Bedfordshire. Ian Feuer is an American-born goalkeeper who played in both Belgium and England, as well as playing for the USA in the early 1990s. Kelvin remembers that he was 6'7". Ian joined LA Galaxy as assistant manager in 2007. Juergen Sommer is probably best known to fans in England for having played 66 games for Queens Park Rangers in the mid-1990s. He also played 10 games for the USA national team.

....

Kelvin turned pro in July 1994 and in September 1994 he was loaned to Torquay United as a replacement for their injured goalkeeper Ashley Bayes. On 22 September 1994, in the *Plainmoor Diary* feature in the *Herald Express* in Torquay, sports reporter David Thomas wrote about the young Kelvin, particularly in games against Colchester United and Wimbledon, the latter in the League Cup.

Thomas related how highly Kelvin was thought of by his manager, David Pleat, and he also quoted the Torquay manager at the time, Don O'Riordan, *"I knew within minutes of the session starting on Friday that David Pleat was right. Kelvin has a tremendous physique and already carries himself like a young man. He's got all the makings of a great 'keeper'".*

The report also gives an insight into just how supportive Geoff and Lilian were to their son in those early days. *"Davis's family showed the family spirit by driving him down on Thursday night – one in his car, one on their own – so he would be rested for training on Friday".*

But a little known fact about Kelvin emerges in David Thomas's article who writes: *"The Welsh FA have tried to persuade Davis to declare his allegiance to them for international purposes, but the Bedford-born youngster has plumped for England".*

It seemed that the family thought that a grandmother of Kelvin (his Nan) had been born in Tonypandy. However, without the evidence of a birth certificate for Nan, Kelvin remained English, as he wanted to.

It is perhaps just as well that he did reject Wales given the spat he had with the ground staff in the warm up for a Saints game at Swansea City when they all but forked through Kelvin's boots before the game.

As it turned out his only experience of playing for England was for the under-21s in June 1995 in the Toulon tournament. He played in round 1 in a game against Angola – England won 1-0. He was playing for Luton at the time and found himself in the company of other of up-and-coming players, such as David Beckham, Phil Neville and future Saint Dean Richards.

....

In June 1995 at Luton he agreed what was to be a three-year contract with David Pleat. However, after the meeting and realising he was *"very green behind the ears"* Kelvin started to wonder if he should have agreed to it. He was established in the team and although he was still very young he felt that he might have undervalued himself, even though the agreement with David Pleat would see him getting another £100 a week – a very good deal at the time.

The following week after he had verbally agreed but did not sign the new three-year contract, David Pleat left Luton and went to manage Sheffield Wednesday.

Shortly after his departure Kelvin received a phone call from David Kohler (the chairman of Luton Town FC from 1992 to 1999). He was concerned because the new contract had not been signed and Kelvin sensed that the chairman had a fear – never substantiated – that Sheffield Wednesday might make an approach for him through David Pleat.

Imagine the scenario: Kelvin is taking a call from the chairman no less in his Mum and Dad's kitchen. David Kohler got straight to the point, *"Kelvin, David Kohler here, I understand there's a contract here you haven't signed yet".*

"No, I haven't".

"Why not?"

"Well, if I'm honest David, I'm not quite sure that it's the right amount of money". Bold though he was he still says that he felt very embarrassed talking like that.

Kelvin's Mum had been washing up and his Dad had been making coffee but the kitchen fell still and silent with all ears on Kelvin's end of the conversation. His Dad looked over at him with an expression that strongly conveyed his doubt that Kelvin had a clue what he was doing.

David Kohler asked, *"What would make you come in and sign this contract?"*

Kelvin gave the honest reply, *"Well, I think another £100 a week".*

The immediate reply was, *"Okay I'll have that in the contract tomorrow. Pop in and sign it".*

Kelvin put the phone down and recalls thinking that it was as if he had made a million pounds in a five-minute conversation. He was going to get another £100 a week, twice the rise that he had agreed with David Pleat.

However, his second lesson on negotiating was yet to unfold. He went to the office the next day to discover that he had to sign a *four-year* contract, not the three-year contract he had been expecting.

Kelvin certainly had grown up when it came to the business of football and he realised that he would need help in the future to deal with contracts.

He now reflects quietly, *"We talk about clubs being afraid of agents and putting the wall up in the face of agents. Don't get me wrong, they haven't all been good for the game but at the same time I think the game has benefitted from them. Also, we talk about the money they take from the game. I don't agree with the amount agents get paid but then clubs pay them and it seems to be that that's how the industry works".*

....

He holds fond memories of his time at Luton Town and their paths would cross again when the Saints played them in the FA Cup in January 2010. Sadly, this was at a time when they were non-league and Kelvin had been away from the club for such a long time and obviously knew none of the players. He says that the match against his old club held no special significance for him because it was a lot different to the club that he had left.

He does admit that he had looked forward to the opportunity of going back to Kenilworth Road and playing them in the league. But he missed out on it because Bart Bialkowski played. So, he has never been back and played at Luton.

Crossing paths with former clubs and with former team mates is not uncommon for footballers and Kelvin has crossed paths with a number of players and former clubs.

When he was at Wimbledon he played with Jason Euell who in August 2007 came to Southampton, via Charlton Athletic and Middlesbrough. Kelvin got on really well with Jason who he considered to be a great addition to the dressing room. *"A very good pro, a very good player. He was fantastic to have at the club".*

Kelvin also played at Wimbledon with David Connolly and they ended up playing together again when David joined the Saints in October 2009.

One match that Kelvin and David played in together was Wimbledon away to Norwich in the (then) Football League Division 1. It was 22 December 2001 and Norwich won 2-1 with David Connolly scoring from the penalty spot for Wimbledon. The goal came just six minutes after Kelvin had been shown a red card and Norwich had scored a penalty.

As Kelvin recalls the Norwich red card was *"an interesting one"*. Norwich City had a player on loan from Wimbledon – a Danish striker called David Nelson – and, unusually, he was allowed to play. The attitude of his parent club was that if he is not good enough for us, then surely we should be happy to play against him. He was a striker who could cause all sorts of trouble and Kelvin says he was prone to go down very easily in the box which he did on this occasion. Following the challenge, the ball came rolling through to Kelvin and he scooped it up. As he walked forward clutching the ball, the referee blew his whistle and awarded a penalty. Kelvin threw the ball in the direction of Nelson and called his name, *"David"*, as he did so. He did it out of frustration and it was certainly not meant to be aggressive. As Kelvin says, *"I know that I could have thrown the ball harder and a lot more aggressively but I didn't."* When he turned he saw the referee go to his pocket and immediately Kelvin feared the worst and he was shown the red card. Kelvin has since met the referee involved who has admitted that nowadays he would probably not send a player off for such behaviour.

At Wimbledon Kelvin played with several well-known players including Neal Ardley, Gareth Ainsworth, Patrick Agyemang, former Saint Neil Shipperley, Nigel Reo-Coker and Jamaican midfielder Jobi Macanuff. He also played with former Welsh international turned TV pundit John Hartson at both Wimbledon and, before that, at Luton Town.

....

Continuing with the theme of 'crossing paths' Kelvin went back with the Saints to Hartlepool United where he had been on loan. However, the match on 24 November 2009 – which the Saints won 3-1 – turned out to be a painful experience for him.

The Saints team had trained at a non-league ground on a really heavy pitch and he admits that he felt a little twinge during the morning but, as Kelvin puts it, players *"go into games and play with little niggles all the time".* In the second half Kelvin found himself kicking into an exceptionally strong wind.

He describes the moment that he ripped an abductor on his left side, an 8-cm tear that went across rather than downwards as might usually be the case. *"I was actually striking the ball pretty well. I ended up putting a bit more into the kick and put my head down, put my foot through the ball and boom, just felt it straightaway. I haven't had too many injuries and that was probably my first experience of a muscle injury. Sometimes you might think you can carry on with whatever it was, but no, it was that instant and I knew it was serious".*

But the positive news was that Kelvin was back on the pitch within six weeks which is regarded as a good recovery for that kind of injury, no doubt because of his overall fitness and his tendency to work hard.

....

For Kelvin, Ipswich Town was *"a fantastic club".* He uses phrases like *"massive club"* and *"a special place".* He had the feeling that it was *"a proper football club".* The facilities they had, compared with what he had experienced before, meant that it came as a big step up for him. People justifiably perceive Ipswich as a friendly club in the same way as they do Southampton, although Kelvin is typically quick to point out that being friendly should not be regarded as a weakness.

When he was there former Saint Jim Magilton was a player, along with Darren Bent and Jermaine Wright, the latter eventually coming to the Saints.

In his time at Ipswich they had two successful seasons, finishing in the play-offs on both occasions and on a particularly limited budget. Kelvin was already pondering the following season when he had a phone call from Joe Royle two days after the season had finished. Joe told Kelvin that Ipswich had received an offer from Premier

League Sunderland and the offer had been accepted. Mick McCarthy was going to call Kelvin shortly and the advice from Joe was to *"listen to what he's got to say".*

Royle who Kelvin regarded as a *"very personal manager"* said, "Mate, I'd love to keep you but we need the money". Darren Bent and Shefki Kuqi were also going because Ipswich needed the cash to be able to strengthen their squad.

....

His experience at Ipswich was a strong contrast with what would come at Sunderland. In terms of playing football at Ipswich there was a strong spirit among team mates. It was not unreasonable to expect that another club, especially following their recent promotion, would have the same feeling in the dressing room and around the club.

Over the years Kelvin has discovered that he likes to work in a positive atmosphere, which he could not feel at Sunderland. As he puts it, *"I just felt that there was a black cloud over the whole place".* Some of his performances were not as strong as they had been in previous seasons even though he probably had his best pre-season period in his career.

However, when Sunderland played at home against Charlton Athletic in the opening game they lost 3-1 with his former team mate Darren Bent scoring twice.

"I'd been working with Bent two years before and we always used to do an afternoon shooting session on a Thursday so I was always confident coming up against him. I knew his technique. I knew that he was a very good striker. It was actually a goal where he got put through one on one, on the angle. I've come out and he's lifted it over me and the ball just brushed my thigh and it's gone over me and into the goal. It was that contact and I thought, have I done enough there, have I saved that? But it went in". In hindsight, that first goal that he conceded pretty much summed up the season for him.

Another player connection for him was when Rory Delap signed from Southampton. Kelvin has only one memory of Rory – a game against Everton in which Rory scored, bearing in mind that Sunderland had not won for weeks. Rory then hit an absolutely wonderful strike that struck the inside of the post, ran across the goal line but failed to go into the net.

One positive side of Kelvin in that period, according to his wife Kelly, is that he would not hide, although this perhaps meant that he became something of a scapegoat. He was always prepared to give interviews but he never blamed anyone, as is his way. Despite some good performances at Sunderland – including a man of the match award that passed almost unnoticed – the season seemed to be painted differently.

Following one match against Manchester United Kelvin found himself being compared with Edwin Van de Saar. The pundits even used evidence to make their own criticism fit but the lesson for Kelvin was to understand the difference between your own self-analysis and pundit analysis.

....

It is only possible to scan through the footballing side of the ten seasons in which Kelvin has served the Saints so loyally. The following chapter looks at key moments both on and off the pitch, recognising that reporting every game would not only be tedious but would probably produce a book that would need to run to several volumes.

Some of the matches covered will be reported in more detail, together with observations from some of the players taking part, in *Match of the New Millennium* that will be published by Hagiology Publishing in August 2016 to coincide with the 15th anniversary of the first game at St Mary's stadium.

Ten Seasons

Before describing specific matches and events it is useful to know how Kelvin reflects on his reasons for staying with the Saints. It is not in his nature to *"fill anyone's head with rubbish"* and to try to suggest that Southampton Football Club – as good as it is – was his sole reason for staying so long. Of course the club is a major part of his presence for so long but as much as anything else it was about happiness for the family and retaining what he calls the *"family infrastructure"*.

Kelvin uses the words *"family"* and *"happy"* a lot (frequently in the same sentence) as he reflects on what is important to him in life. As described earlier he had known unhappiness during his season in Sunderland and he didn't want that to be repeated. It is difficult to avoid clichés such as *"You can't put a price on happiness"* or *"Money can't buy you happiness"* to convey how Kelvin feels.

His decision not to move to West Ham United in the summer of 2009 was not easy. The money on offer at West Ham was considerably more than Southampton could offer once the club had a new owner. But, the wages that Southampton were offering were not, as Kelvin puts it, *"breadline wages"*. He does not boast a highly extravagant lifestyle and likes to see himself as a *"saver"* – which is probably just as well given that he is a goalkeeper. With his financial advisor, Duncan, who is also a close friend, he has achieved what he wants which is *"to set aside enough to make sure the family is comfortable"*.

He does not deny that several factors influenced his decision to stay at Southampton and these are all things that have fed his passion in differing degrees. It is important to him to be living in an area that is *"a fantastic place to live and to bring up a family"* and to be only an hour and 40 minutes to drive to see his parents and other family and friends.

When he decided to come back from West Ham his friend and advisor met him in Bishops Waltham with a copy of a contract faxed from Southampton. He did not hesitate to sign. And when he drove back to Southampton he felt physically lighter with the stress of uncertainty lifted.

He felt that at Southampton he did not have to climb over any obstacle in order to go and simply to do the job that he loves. *"For me it was about going into a fantastic working environment and doing what I really, really enjoyed".* He reflects with pride on the fact that the decision to stay with the Saints has led to so much happiness and success, especially for those who are dearest to him. He hopes that he has built platforms for his family's future contentment and for his children to realise their dreams. Those who know him would say that it is certainly a reality and not merely a hope.

....

Kelvin made his debut for the Saints in the first match of the 2006-07 season – a 2-2 draw away at Derby County on 6 August 2006. There was a curious symmetry to his first season as a Saint given that the final game of the season was also against Derby County, the crucial second leg of the Championship semi-final play-off.

The first leg at St. Mary's ended with a 2-1 win for Derby but Kelvin was not in goal for that game, having been out with an injury picked up in a game at Cardiff City two months earlier. Although he had got fit again Kelvin knew that *"George Burley liked Bart (Bialkowski) as a keeper and throughout his managerial career he had always given opportunities to young goalkeepers".* Kelvin respected the fact that Burley wanted to give Bart a run.

He came in for the second leg which finished 3-2 in favour of the Saints, meaning that the sides were 4-4 on aggregate. Saints had scored more away goals but unfortunately in this contest they did not count double, a source of pain for the club and the travelling supporters in the kind of foul weather that well reflected their mood.

It meant that Kelvin was left with the unenviable task of facing a penalty shoot-out that could effectively determine whether the club would remain in the Championship or whether it would play at Wembley in the play-off final that could bring promotion to the Premier League.

Kelvin describes facing penalties as giving rise to a mix of emotions, *"excitement, opportunity and also a little bit of fear".* It is a responsibility that is the culmination of what a player has trained and worked for and knows that just one action could determine so much. In open play there is no real thinking time when having to make a save but, in contrast, with a penalty there is the time to focus on the fact that you are about to have to make a save.

Of the game itself, played on a very rainy evening in Derby, Kelvin recalls several moments. There was a quite high ball that almost slipped through his grasp, making him think that it might have not gone his way and it would have been a different evening. Then *"Bestie"* (Leon Best) scored an own goal when, instead of heading the ball, he got his leg up and it came off his toe and hooked into the far corner.

Jon Viafara who was not renowned for being a goal scorer, scored an amazing goal which put the Saints 2-1 up and Kelvin remembers thinking that could be enough.

Let Kelvin talk through the first penalty:

"I changed my mind on the penalty...he goes to my left and I go to my right. I can tell you that until he struck that ball I was going to go to my left. When I look back I think that was the only one where I thought if I had gone the right way I would have saved it. If I talk about disappointment, then again that's something of a lesson – that is to listen to your gut feeling".

From that unfortunate lesson he decided that for every penalty that came afterwards in his career he was not going to change his mind. Kelvin explains that, regardless of whether he makes a save or not, he has to live with his decision. If he goes with his gut feeling he knows that he could have done no better, but if he changes his mind it leaves him questioning himself for a long time in the future.

Kelvin was standing to the side of the goal when Inigo Idiakez put his penalty wide. He felt the pain of his team mate especially with him being a former Derby player but the disappointment of the Saints fans was palpable given that the penalties were taken at their end. The Derby fans invaded the pitch but the image of Idiakez with his head down in the rain walking past jubilant Derby players will long remain in the memory for Kelvin, his fellow players and the supporters.

Being so close to the fans on this occasion allowed Kelvin to feel their real disappointment. Sometimes, but not on this occasion, the spectators behind the goal can take opportunities to vent their feelings at the goalkeeper. This applies to fans from both sides and goalkeepers always have to remain calm when bad insults are flying in.

....

However, Kelvin found it impossible not to react when a small group of Saints supporters immediately behind the goal decided to take out their feelings on him. The match was against Sheffield Wednesday away in November 2007, six months after the Derby County match and with Kelvin now well into his second season.

In terms of trying to get his Saints career really moving Kelvin always felt that there was a hangover from losing the play-off at Derby. He was trying to brush that aside and to get on with his new life and not let it get him down in a way that can spill over to your whole life, including the family. He seemed to be making ground and had put in some good performances. He was getting on both with his job and with looking for a house where the family could settle.

The Sheffield Wednesday match was not exactly memorable for Saints followers – or perhaps it was memorable for the wrong reasons – the Saints lost 5-0. But it was probably a turning point for Kelvin and his relationship with the fans.

Whether consciously or not Kelvin has forgotten much of what happened for the goals, except for a couple of them. He describes one as *"one of those strikes where the centre forward just put his head down and smacked it. I tried to get something in the way of it and I think it passed between my legs and my arm and it managed to just find its way in".* It was one of those strikes that makes a goalkeeper wonder how the shot got past without touching any part of his anatomy.

Then he was beaten again and he thinks that was probably the fifth goal, which was conceded with the Saints fans right behind him. Anyone who has been to Hillsborough knows that supporters located at the front of the lower tier behind the goal are close to the goalkeeper.

Kelvin struggles to remember the goals but he can remember as clear as day what happened after the fifth went in. Substitute Bart Bialkowski was warming up on the side lines and some of the Saints fans started singing his name. Kelvin felt, *"it really went through me, really wound me up".* He is definitely not hot-headed and his wife Kelly confirms that he remains very calm until things reach a certain point.

Notwithstanding his usual calmness and professionalism, the jeers from his own fans at Sheffield Wednesday made him lose his cool. He says that *"a little switch went in my head"* and he thought to himself that he was not going to put up with the chanting. So he turned and told them *"eff off".*

He remembers that after the match some people claimed he had said something else but he is adamant that he never abused any individual personally. Saying *"eff off"* was enough for him to show how he was feeling. He can also remember that there was a small section of the crowd that rushed forward as if they wanted to take his head off and with his usual candour he admits, *"I'd have been quite up for the fight to be honest".*

But Kelvin had his attention directed away from the abuse because there was a group in the crowd that gave *"a little jeer"* and gave a cry of *"Hey"*, as if wanting to convey that he was one of them. It seemed that there were some supporters who felt his reaction was justified and as Kelvin puts it, *"I think from that day in a strange way a bit of a barrier went down between myself and the fans".* It seemed that a majority of Saints fans felt that the guys behind the goal were out of order since Kelvin actually showed that he was not aloof and that he too cared about what happened in the game.

The club strongly encouraged him to write an apology but with characteristic honesty he admits that he did not want to write it. This was not out of disrespect for the club or the fans but, on the contrary, it was a moment that made him think that the fans gained a bit more respect for him and he gained more respect for them.

Minor altercations with the crowd or with fans are not unusual. As a goalkeeper Kelvin is only too aware of this although sometimes the banter from fans can be more amusing than hostile. People care about their football club and some are predisposed to share their feelings in a passionate and loud manner. As with their opinions of officials some fans seem to make it personal with the target of their anger and frustration.

The key for Kelvin is knowing how to react in a calm way so as not to exacerbate the situation, one example coming early in Kelvin's Saints career in September 2006 when he and his Dad were walking across the car park at St. Mary's and a fan approached him. He smiles as he says that he should really know the name of the fan who still comes to every game, including all the away games and is known to say 'hello' to Geoff. The fan started walking next to him and asked, *"What the hell's going on?"* and various other foul-mouthed taunts.

According to Kelvin any player in any sport will tell you that immediately after a game is probably not the best time to enter into a critical discussion. So Kelvin simply turned round to his Dad and said *"Dad, get him away from me."* He knew that he was boiling up but he did not want to do anything rash. His Dad is calmer and simply asked the offending fan to give Kelvin a bit of room, saying, *"Leave him alone, he's doing his best".*

This incident occurred after the Saints had been beaten at home 2-1 by QPR on 30 September 2006, the day after Kelvin's 30th birthday. Together with close friends and team mates Kelly had secretly organised a surprise party for Kelvin but he was so despondent about the result that he steadfastly refused to leave the house, saying he was not in any mood to go out, celebrate and enjoy himself. It took much cajoling and arm-twisting by family and friends to get him to go out, much to Kelly's eventual delight. If anyone ever doubted his commitment, his bad mood if the team loses and the nearly-lost birthday party is evidence to the contrary.

In November 2007 Kelvin returned to his former club, Ipswich Town, the match also marking the return of former Ipswich manager George Burley and Malcolm Webster. The Saints lost 2-0 but Kelvin reflects less on the result than on his feelings when he returned to the club where he had been so happy.

Although it was tough for him Kelvin characteristically felt more for George and Malcolm who were also returning for the first time and had to take the brunt of the banter and abuse.

Kelvin felt that he had always had a good connection with the fans at Ipswich, being voted player of the season in the Championship. A very small group of fans started singing *"You're just a greedy b******"* because of his move to Sunderland. But it was probably only one per cent of the fans behind the goal who were singing and the others got *"straight on their case",* as Kelvin calls it. He considered the reaction of the majority of the Ipswich fans as a real sign of respect.

He feels that supporters who sing such things do not necessarily have insights into the real story. Just because a player has left their club they assume it was for money and entirely for their own personal gain.

Kelvin reflects on this, *"I can understand the sense of responsibility of a player. You've played in a team, you've been part of a team, and you've been relegated. I do think a player needs to take a personal responsibility for that and almost take the responsibility to get the club back to where they were. Everybody knows now the difference between the Premier League and the Championship. Most fans can understand when it's honest and open and they're respectful when a player will explain a situation".*

Or, as Kelly puts it succinctly, *"The negatives are always louder than the positives".*

....

2007-08 had started reasonably well with two wins and a draw in the first six games. And this year was to be a happier birthday for Kelvin, winning 2-1 away to Sheffield United on 29 September 2007 – his 31st birthday.

But three days later on a bitter cold Tuesday evening it was something of a disaster away at Preston. The Saints lost 5-1 and the Saints' goal was even an own goal. To add insult to injury the scorer of two goals was Patrick Agyemang.

....

In February 2008 Kelvin first became acquainted with a man that would become a close friend and a Saints legend to boot: Rickie Lambert. But this was not necessarily the way that Kelvin might have wanted to start a new relationship. Rickie scored the only goal, the winner, when the Saints played Bristol Rovers away in the FA Cup.

Playing down the quality of the free kick from Rickie, Kelvin claims that he was right behind it but it took a slight deflection off Jermaine Wright's backside, although Rickie says it went off Wright's shin. It is hardly a defence for the poor result but Kelvin did make one good save against Rickie in the first half, down at his feet.

John Gorman and Jason Dodd were in charge and it was a period of time when the Saints needed to get wins. It hurts players and fans to go out of a cup but getting knocked out of the FA Cup by lower league opposition can sometimes act as a warning of what is to come. This result heralded the start of a period that might lead to relegation, although that would still be another season away.

At that time the Saints had just signed a new central defender and Kelvin recalls him publicly criticising the team in the press. He made comments along the lines that a few players needed to look in the mirror. As ever Kelvin was mindful of the effect this could have on the team and that *"it didn't do the dressing room much good"*. Kelvin's view is that unless a player is self-critical when he does an interview it will always look as if he is trying to deflect blame onto others. He is clear that, if there is discontent, it becomes an additional pressure to deal with and it creates a fear that the team is not only up against eleven players on the pitch.

....

It has been known for players to blame a poor result, such as the surprising cup exit at Bristol Rovers, on the facilities (or lack of them) at a stadium. But, as those who know him might expect, Kelvin takes the opposite view, *"I used to find that the worse the ground I was playing at, the more I wanted to show that it did not affect me".*

Having played football in what he describes as *"magnificent stadiums"* Kelvin knew that, when called on to play in a more modest stadium, there would be players who would be thinking that they were too good for that kind of setting. But Kelvin admits that such an attitude *"got under his skin".*

In this sort of situation, it is that tough attitude in Kelvin that comes to the fore and why he says that he was never afraid to play in League One. He never once thought ill of any club for their less luxurious facilities. He simply experienced a strong motivation to go out and show that he could cope with playing in such an environment. It is not in his nature to show disrespect for clubs like Carlisle, Hartlepool or Rochdale, although he admits that self-motivation did not work well at Rochdale where the Saints lost.

There is one ground where the starting 11 go into the dressing room and when they vacate it the substitutes go in to change. Even this could not faze Kelvin and, similarly, he would just smile when the team went into a dressing room to find a little puddle on the cold concrete floor. Kelvin admits that *"it used to make me have a little smile"* and he was determined not to let it affect him or his performance.

....

2008-09 was not a good season for several reasons but it serves to demonstrate the resilience of Kelvin and his insistence on not solely celebrating the high points and good times in his ten seasons at Southampton. He is brave enough to share the low points that he lived through with such continuing commitment.

The season started badly with two defeats on the trot and there was only one win in the first seven games.

Kelvin recalls that the players were left surprised and a little confused by a couple of things that occurred in the close season – not excuses in themselves for the poor showing on the pitch but important context for the season.

The players thought that Nigel Pearson had done well enough to continue in the post of manager. He seemed to have proved himself to be a good manager and there was a sense that he could be at Southampton for some years. Kelvin stresses that *"he came in on his own and with no staff and he didn't just grab the dressing room he grabbed the club by the throat".* Nigel took control and was a very engaging man who gained a lot of respect in a short time from players, staff and, significantly from the supporters. As Kelvin adds, *"To this day people that worked with him at the club still speak highly of him. It's quite rare to only have a manager for such a short time".*

In addition to hearing about the departure of Nigel Pearson the players all got a phone call while they were on holiday to tell them to report back a week earlier. For footballers the close season is a precious time and the Saints had got to the end of the previous season just managing to stay up. The early call back came as a blow as it coincided with the players learning that Nigel Pearson had been replaced by Jan Poortvliet and Mark Wotte. They were perceived as a double act, leading to corny headlines about 'double Dutch', but, it was clear that Poortvliet was the manager.

On the pitch there was a total change of style of play although Kelvin makes the observation that it is *"a little bit like how the game is now. The way they were looking to play was probably ten years too soon".*

It looked like a brave decision and the policy was that young players would play. Other players, Kelvin included, will assert that it is not about age, it is about being good enough and with the right skills regardless of how old or young a player is. There was a growing perception among the players that the policy was largely influenced by financial considerations. Whether it was strictly true or not, there was a feeling that players were not always starting games on ability but because they were the right age and in the right wage bracket.

The Saints played in the opening game at Cardiff City with a very immature team and, according to Kelvin, they played a lot of balls in their own half and he recalls playing balls in and around the six-yard box. This led to the opposition staying high up the pitch and not allowing the long ball.

Playing with young players did not appear to be conducive to winning, especially given that the front men at that time did not command high levels of respect from their opponents. Of course, there were some very talented but inexperienced youngsters, such as David McGoldrick and Adam Lallana, but as Kelvin puts it now *"We never really got going that season".*

....

For the supporters the alarm bells started ringing loudly when the Saints lost 4-1 away at QPR. Patrick Agyemang popped up with a goal to haunt Kelvin again and former Saint Dexter Blackstock got two. Loftus Road is never a good ground to go to but losing 4-1 was distressing especially with the experienced players who were on the bench, such as Chris Perry and Stern John. Kelvin recalls that the result was not helped by an offside decision that was a massive turning point in the game, together with young Ollie Lancashire being sent off.

Two 2-0 wins against Doncaster Rovers away and at home to Norwich City proved only to be a false dawn. It was six weeks before another victory came, 3-2 away at Preston which in some way atoned for the result there the previous season but which meant little in the overall scheme of things. What Kelvin recalls of that game is Dave McGoldrick's fantastic winner but he goes on to reflect, *"We had some very good players but we weren't getting enough goals".*

The lost and drawn games outnumbered the wins but the next significant game for Kelvin was a 3-0 win away to Ipswich Town. It was significant simply because it was the first time that he was on the winning side on a return to Portman Road. Kelvin's former team mate at Wimbledon Jason Euell scored twice. However, this too proved to be a false dawn with the next game away at Birmingham City resulting in a 1-0 defeat.

Mark Wotte had taken charge and the first thing he did was to have a meeting with the more senior pros to see what was needed. As a result, the experienced lads came back into the side and although Stern John was out on loan Paul Wotton was in the team and the side seemed more solid.

However, the Saints only recorded one win in the remaining 11 games that followed the victory at Ipswich Town and, consequently, they were relegated to League One.

Kelvin was on the list of players that were in a certain wage bracket and were likely to be released or sold. Partly as a result of this the club signed Tommy Forecast. In the pre-season there were two games in one day, one in Winchester and one in Basingstoke. The first team went to Basingstoke and won 9-0. Kelvin played in the other team which went to Winchester. After the Basingstoke match the management team returned to watch the game at Winchester. In terms of the style they wanted to play, especially with good distribution from the back, Kelvin felt that he had a good game and consequently he kept his place. The chairman Rupert Lowe indicated that he wanted to keep Kelvin for the following season. However, whilst he expected him to remain at the club Lowe made it clear that he would not be in a position to offer the kind of money that Kelvin had been earning until then.

....

Kelvin has always had a good standing in the dressing room where he is almost always a calming influence but he got tipped over the edge near the end of the season in which they were facing relegation to League One. The Saints played at Sheffield Wednesday – there seems to be something about playing there that brings out the worst in Kelvin!

At half time the Saints were 1-0 down and although they had the likes of Rudi Skacel and Adam Lallana, according to Kelvin it was *"not a strong Saints side".* Jan Paul Saeijs was a centre half who was on loan from a Dutch club called Roda JC but Kelvin felt that the otherwise good defender was having a *"horrendous game".* A win would have taken the Saints out of the bottom three and Kelvin admits that his frustration was fuelled by the team showing *"very little effort".* The pressure got to him because he knew that if the Saints lost the game the chances of us staying up were going to be very slim.

He recalls thinking about the consequences of the club being relegated. He was in the last year of his contract and in the likely event of the club not being able to offer him a contract that would mean *"moving to another club, moving the family, taking the kids out of school"* – disrupting everything that he holds dear outside football.

Kelvin went into the dressing room at half time, completely *"flipping my lid. I ended up having a bit of a scream and shout".* He describes how he felt heavily disappointed and let down and the anger and the pressure just got to him. At one point he can remember turning round, looking a couple of lads in the eyes and *"seeing Andrew Surman and Dave McGoldrick looking at me – I don't' know whether it was surprise or fear or what".*

Having suddenly realised that he had gone too far by losing his temper he tells how he went into the shower cubicle and just tried to get his *"head straight".* Keith Granger followed him in and said a few words that helped him to reset his focus on the game, knowing that they had to play the second half.

The Saints lost the game and Kelvin sensed that it was a nail in the coffin but it was the eventual reduction of points that *"killed us completely".* He remembers sitting in the cafeteria at the training ground and watching that news come up and everyone looking at each other as much to say *"Well, that's that then."*

....

Burnley was the last home game of the season and Kelvin recalls the chaos that ensued when there was a pitch invasion after the game. Close to the end of the game his team mate Paul Wotton was injured and managed to pick up the nickname *"gums"* because, as Kelvin describes it, *"He went up for a header in the last minute of the game and one of the centre halves for Burnley came right through the back of him and caught him, completely unintentionally, with the back of his arm and knocked his front teeth out. He was still laying in a mess on the pitch when everyone came running on. I can remember attempting to get to him. I think it was Keith who sent me in and we went and picked him up off the floor".*

....

Both relegation *and* administration came and all the players and staff could do was watch the press and news reports to try to work out what was going to happen. It is no exaggeration to say that none of the players could really imagine what was to come.

In such dark times for everyone associated with Southampton Football Club it is heartening to hear Kelvin relate an incident that is amusing now, although it was undoubtedly serious at the time.

The players were invited to a meeting with the administrator. It was at a time when Rupert Lowe and others could have no say in the future of the club so the administrator decided to meet and speak to the players directly. It all seemed very formal with a long table in the meeting room. The administrator stood at one end heading up the meeting, Kelvin was seated in the middle on one side and Paul Wotton was near the end of the table opposite the administrator.

The administrator talked about their emerging plans and how they were going to turn the club round. The first example of what was being explored was their view that the club was not fully exploiting the potential advertising space of the stadium. He explained that St Mary's sits under a flight path, as if Kelvin and the others had not noticed. The proposition was that there should be advertising on top of the stand which would be visible to the passengers of the planes passing over. The second idea was to install an indoor golf simulator in the back of one of the stands. Before he could unfold the next idea he was interrupted by Paul Wotton, *"That's all very well, mate, but when are we effin getting paid?"*

Although footballers are far from being badly paid, they are not all multi-millionaires and they have lifestyle commitments which reflect their incomes. If that income dries up they are as vulnerable as anyone in terms of paying mortgages and bringing up their families. Let us pause for tears of compassion!

Seriously though, the interjection from Paul Wotton clearly echoed the thoughts of his team mates – in the real world their personal priorities surpassed the well-meant visions and ideas of the administrator.

....

The new season 2009-10 was greeted by supporters of Southampton with mixed feelings. On the one hand there was a sense of despondency about having to watch the Saints play in League One but on the other hand there was elation at the fact that their club would be playing at all. In August 2009 Southampton Football Club had been saved by the late Markus Liebherr and the club was able to turn the page and look forwards.

In addition to everything that had happened over the summer of 2009 the supporters were buoyed by the fact that Kelvin Davis was still at the club. All sorts of rumours abounded as to why and how Kelvin stayed but the bottom line is that Kelvin decided to turn down the riches of Premier League football at West Ham United and remain where he and his family were happy.

His good friend Paul Wotton recalls, *"I actually saw him that day. We took the kids to a play park when he came back. It just didn't sit right with him. That sums up the man. He was part of the relegation team but it was nothing to do with him because he was outstanding. He wanted to get back up, get promoted to the Championship and ultimately the Premier League and that's what he's done".*

....

For many supporters 2009-10 was a season in which they could visit new grounds that housed clubs in League One. But mention 2009-10 to anyone connected with the Saints and it will not fail to bring back memories of the one outstanding visit for supporters in that season: Wembley Stadium on 28 March 2010.

The story of the 4-1 victory over Carlisle United in the final of the Johnstone's Paint Trophy has been told over and over again and does not need to be repeated here. While there are detractors who wish to remind Saints supporters that it is not a major trophy, a visit to a Wembley final had been far from everyone's minds in July 2009.

Kelvin says his main recollection is the red-and-white sea of fans who had travelled from the south coast and from all over the country.

"Having such a massive magnitude of Saints fans turn up for that game, lifting the trophy was a very special – a very, very special – moment. And looking at, and seeing all the Saints fans there – we could have filled the place if we had the opportunity to. To look up and three-quarters of your eye-line is filled with Saints fans and knowing that my family were there and my friends were there, I think anyone who has ever been in that position can understand. And people mention that it was the Paint Trophy, it wasn't the FA Cup and it wasn't the League Cup. I can understand that but to us at that time and for 55,000 Saints fans – or whatever it was – it didn't matter what cup it was. It was a fantastic day."

Kelvin's father-in-law, Pat Greening, remembers, *"When Kelvin came out to warm up the noise was awesome and that was just for the goalkeepers".*

Everyone has their own memories of that day, none more so than Kelly Davis. Caring so much as he does about the happiness of his wife and family Kelvin admits that because they were being so well looked after by the club it meant that he and the other players had one less thing to worry about.

Kelly describes how the players' families stayed at one hotel where family rooms meant that they could stay together with their children. They all travelled together by coach, reflecting and strengthening a real community spirit that Kelly says existed for the wives, girlfriends and families. Because they were seated together in one area of the stadium the players knew exactly where their families were. Kelly remembers Kelvin looking up and pointing and waving at the children.

With regards to the game Kelly says that *"winning like that was really nice because often in games you win by one goal and you're on eggshells and you don't really enjoy the game until you look back on it. But I enjoyed the game because we were winning by such a margin".*

Kelly was told about the hundreds of people who came down to the game from Leighton Buzzard, wanting to support both Kelvin and the Saints. By all accounts the trains from Bedfordshire and Buckinghamshire were packed with Saints fans in their red and white.

One image that sticks in the minds of both Kelvin and Kelly, and undoubtedly in the minds of everyone else who was there, is that of a smiling Markus Liebherr leaning back in the royal box with his small digital camera so that he could get a photo of every player as they collected their medals and the trophy.

Kelly has a vivid and proud memory of her husband and club captain Kelvin lifting the trophy, with the assistance of Dean Hammond who was team captain for the match. Other than that she admits that many of her memories are from pictures taken on the day.

One memory that sticks out for Kelvin and some of his team mates including Dan Harding and Paul Wotton is something that might not have registered with many people in the crowd. Papa Waigo seemed not to understand the convention of the trophy presentation and can be seen in photos pushing his way along the line of team mates awaiting their medals in order to grab the trophy. He did not realise that it would be passed down the line. Dan Harding, who was immediately behind Kelvin, remembers saying *"What's he doing?"*

To say that Papa was really excited is an understatement as Paul Wotton describes him, *"a great lad but he didn't really know what was going on at the time. Afterwards he went mad in the dressing-room as well but unfortunately I got called in for a random drug test so I missed all the banter in the changing room".*

When they returned to Southampton all the players and their families (without the children) as well as many staff went for a meal and a party at dock gate 4, Grand Café, and they took the trophy with them. Kelly sums up the mood that evening, *"Probably more than anything it was the start of the way up. You felt the way it was going and we had a really good team as well – better than where we should have been and so much confidence".*

What Kelly omits to say is what happened later but Dan Harding takes up the story.

"When the party finished a number of people went on to another club –called Rosso or something similar. We were all having a really good night until Kelvin decided to pick up Mrs Lambert and run round with her on his shoulder. They [the club owners] didn't like it and all of us got chucked out. I don't think we were being too raucous. Just another one of SKD's actions".

....

Taking into account the Trophy win and the positive feeling about the team's potential, the question on many lips was whether 2010-11 would see the Saints getting back up to the Championship. Kelvin says that the players certainly had no sense of what the season might bring. They even lost the opening game at home 1-0 against Plymouth Argyle.

Kelvin felt the pressure of *"simply being Southampton"* because when the Saints went to any club in that league it was their cup final. This does not imply any disrespect whatsoever to the clubs concerned. When they came to Southampton their reaction would be *"what a fantastic stadium"* and their performances could be lifted.

The chairman at the time wanted to invest in what was important for the players to show that they too were valued. As Kelvin puts it, *"If we did well on the pitch we would be rewarded".* This is why they found themselves having a great pre-season which probably matched anything that Premier League clubs were doing. Kelvin has no hesitation in saying that a massive positive with Nicola Cortese was that he was clear as to what he wanted to create and what he wanted to achieve for the club.

The pre-season trip was away in Switzerland and the squad stayed in Interlaken in what Kelvin calls *"a five-star hotel, and then some".* It was such that the players did not feel that they could go in wearing football boots and dirty kit, so they all almost stripped before going through the hotel to their suites.

The players hired bikes and cycled to training every morning. The club groundsman had been out there to make sure the training pitch was in good condition and a beautiful mountain provided the backdrop. Inspired by being in such a surrounding, the players had more than the usual two- or three-day trip in favour of a week-long camp where everyone was expected to work hard. Most important of all, it was a great opportunity to work and relax together.

They had time in the evening to relax but had to bear in mind that Alan Pardew was very clear about what he expected on his pre-season trips and he wanted no-one getting up to any funny business. The then assistant manager Wally Downes expressed it a little more graphically and despite the joviality the lads got the message. As ever, Kelvin was the spokesperson for the squad and when a 10 o'clock curfew was announced he found himself being poked in the back by David Connolly saying, *"Make it half ten, Make it half ten".* So Kelvin dutifully asked, *"Gaffer, can we make that half ten? Because, I don't know about you but ten o'clock is a bit early".* He knew that Alan Pardew liked to give players responsibility and a little bit of power and he said without hesitation: *"No problem".* He gave them an extra half hour but on a couple of evenings 10.30 turned into 11.30.

One incident that Kelvin remembers happened right in front of him and involved Frazer Richardson who had only recently signed for the club. As Kelvin describes it, *"We were doing a bit of crossing and finishing and someone whipped a ball in to the far post and Frazer did a diving header, headed it out and as he landed right by my feet he dislocated his shoulder. I'm picking him up to his feet and knew instantly it was a bad one. He was in a lot of pain. He'd just signed as well and you don't really know these guys, it was their first trip. I put an arm round him, making sure he was okay".*

The ethos of Southampton Football Club was quickly instilled in new arrivals as evidenced by Danny Butterfield, who had joined the squad but not finally signed his contract. However, there he was collecting balls behind the goal. It must have made him feel like *"a wally really"*, according to Kelvin but Danny, who would become *"a great member of the Saints' dressing room"*, was happy to spend his first few pre-contract days acting as a ball boy (or ball man).

Kelvin reckons it was good management to encourage the lads to enjoy themselves and to let their hair down together away from the limelight, especially with the new squad. All going out together was character building and certainly put the squad in good stead.

Paul Wotton had missed a couple of days of the pre-season trip with a back injury. The squad had all been on a gentle bar-to-bar crawl on their bikes and by the end of the evening they all decided to congregate in the only night club in Interlaken. They all went down the steps and in his own unique way Paul Wotton walked straight onto the dance floor and started to break dance, spinning around on his back and onto his shoulder. When he jumped up onto his feet he looked over and saw the entire coaching staff sitting watching him. It was a revelation as to the healing powers of alcohol when it comes to recovering from a bad back. Paul ended up spending an hour talking to the coaching staff while the other players were unfazed and carried on with their night out.

Another funny incident on the way to the night club involved Dan Harding. The players were all in a jovial mood and were having a bit of a race on their bikes and Dan decided to cut off the corner. Kelvin still remembers it as one of the funniest things he can recall. As Dan cut off the corner he shouted, *"I've got it, I've got it"*, and then he just disappeared. All anyone heard was an almighty splash.

There was a pond on the corner of the pathway and the splash came from Dan. When the others got to him he jumped to his feet looking as if he thought he was dead. He leapt up gasping, his hair soaking wet and his clothes drenched. Kelvin and the others saw that he was alright and just carried on with a cheery wave, *"See you later Dan".* He stomped back to the hotel, dripping wet, got changed and then went straight down to the night club with a fresh set of clothes on.

The postscript to this story came on the airport-bound coach the next day when the manager announced, *"There are some bikes missing".* Kelvin cannot recall whether only eight bikes had been returned or eight bikes were still missing, out of twenty. *"Where are they?"* continued Alan Pardew. There was some sniggering as the team tried not to make eye contact with the manager, and he then said, *"We either find them or they're all coming out your wages".* Of course the players turned to Dan and asked loudly, *"Dan, did you get your bike out of the lake?"*

Anyway, Kelvin managed to negotiate with the club secretary that the money would come out of the first win of the season and he wonders, *"That's perhaps why we didn't win".*

....

Despite admitting that he felt the pressure of *"being Southampton"* the season undoubtedly showed Kelvin at his peak. He was ever-present in the side and recorded 20 clean sheets which is a post-war record for any Southampton goalkeeper.

With the fine for the missing bikes hanging over them the Saints lost the opening game of the season against Plymouth Argyle at the beginning of August. They beat AFC Bournemouth at home in the League Cup but the first win in the league did not come until the fifth game of the season when the Saints beat Bristol Rovers 4-0 away with Rickie Lambert scoring from the penalty spot against his former club. Shortly after the win the manager Alan Pardew was surprisingly sacked.

To add to the angst among the fans Swindon Town came to St Mary's three days later to compete against the holders of the Johnstone's Paint Trophy. It was a bad evening all round with Lee Barnard sent off and the Saints being unceremoniously dumped out in the first round, losing 3-0. Kelvin had to be reminded recently that the scorer of the second goal was one Charlie Austin.

....

On 3 January 2011 the Saints visited a ground that prompts a simple question: how does a team feel when they have to walk the length of the car park at Dagenham and Redbridge, past supporters from both sides just to get to the players' entrance? What a huge contrast to making their way into their five-star hotel in Interlaken.

Kelvin thinks that this might affect some players but as already mentioned he see these situations as a test of his own character. In his mind he suspects that people will be thinking that he will not be able to handle this kind of setting but even before he has kicked a ball his attitude is, *"I'll show you how well I can handle this".*

It's been like that throughout his career, coming from Luton Town and the lower leagues has by no means been a fast rise. He moved to the Premier League at Wimbledon but they had no training ground. They shared a ground and the players had to train in Richmond Park, with people walking their dogs while the team were practising set pieces. He had not had an extravagant upbringing and it was not until the move to Ipswich Town that he started to experience *"that nice atmosphere that is a proper club atmosphere, with a training ground, four or five physios and all that kind of thing. And you were cared for".*

As it happened Dagenham and Redbridge did have a massive changing room but the Saints only played there once because Dagenham and Redbridge got relegated. The Saints won 3-1 with more a large contingency of Saints fans in a total attendance of only 3,582. They occupied the newly-built stand behind the goal and his friend Dan Harding reminds Kelvin that he got chatted up from that stand. A far cry from the incident at Sheffield Wednesday.

Kelvin says that what stuck in his mind most of all was the Dagenham and Redbridge tactic of sending up a long ball from the goalkeeper, for it to be flicked on to a second man running. Nigel Adkins had changed the team for this game and Radhi Jaidi came into the side. Their first goal kick was taken on the wind and then it was kicked in to the edge of the Saints' box and Radhi stuck his left arm up, blocked the run of the centre forward and then headed the ball back to the goalkeeper. I felt the whole crowd just go *"Oooooh!"* It was almost the sound of *"Oooooh"* which actually conveys *"this ain't gonna be our day".* Kelvin adds, *"Radhi went on and played very well, won every header. I only remember him losing one header".*

The other memorable moment from the game was when they had a free kick with the Saints leading 2-1. It was a fantastic free kick that soared over the wall and Kelvin had to go full length for it. It hit the underside of the crossbar and came down and hit Kelvin on the back and then, as he puts it, *"it went splat in a puddle".* It was sitting right on the goal line and Kelvin just scooped it up. Within two minutes the Saints went 3-1 up. It was going to be their day after all.

....

Eight days after Dagenham and Redbridge the Saints went to Oldham Athletic and won 6-0. *"We were unbelievable that night",* just about sums it up from Kelvin. There were six goals from six different players and six players on the pitch who either had or would have full international experience.

Being the sensitive person that he is Kelvin might have had feelings of sympathy that night for the opposition goalkeeper Ben Amos, who was on loan from Manchester United and, unfortunately for Amos, Sir Alex Ferguson was there to watch the match.

Kelvin says that his feelings really depend on who is at the other end. During the match he certainly says an emphatic *"No",* adding *"You feel a little bit like you're in a boxing ring and it's him against you in that respect. You're not going to start thinking whether they're hard done by or feelings at that point".* He acknowledges that considering the way the Saints played that night he was certainly more involved in his own performance and that of the team.

He does admit that he can feel sorry for another keeper. It was before his time at Southampton but he remembers playing against Ludo Mikloško when he was on loan at QPR and they got relegated. Kelvin was still at Wimbledon and can remember thinking *"Poor sod"* because he was getting let down by his players. A man of such experience who had played at a high level and he genuinely felt sorry for him.

....

On 9 April 2011 Saints' supporters virtually took over Brisbane Road, the home of Leyton Orient. The attendance that day was 7,174, nearly 3,000 of which were away supporters. The away fans were housed in the whole of one side of the ground and the noise they made was deafening.

Playing in such an atmosphere with such great expectations, can have both a positive and a negative effect for Kelvin and the other players. In this case the result was positive, the match finishing in a 2-0 win for the Saints.

When a player knows that the team is in a good moment and they are together and playing well the fans can become the 12th man. But, as Kelvin asserts, with the team and the types of players that the Saints had then, they would always be a threat. The likes of Rickie Lambert, Adam Lallana and Jason Puncheon are all players capable of scoring goals.

Reminded that Puncheon did not play that day at Orient Kelvin responds with a grin, *"I wasn't sure whether Punch was coming or going at the time but the bottom line is that he's proved that his ability was never ever in question".*

....

On 23 April 2011 when the Saints went to play Brighton and Hove Albion at the Withdean stadium, it proved to be a memorable game for a number of reasons.

First of all, the home side wanted the Saints to form a guard of honour before the game because Brighton had already won the league. The offer was declined and for the players and staff it was just another fixture and that was that.

Secondly, it seems that something said by Nigel Adkins in the press in the run-up to the game had been blown out of proportion and had upset the Brighton manager.

Thirdly, there were problems with the ball boys. One in particular was taking an inordinate amount of time to return the ball to Kelvin for goal kicks and Nigel Adkins became cross with him at half-time. For those football fans who never went to the Withdean you need to know that the playing area was circled by an eight lane running track and this gave ball boys ample opportunity to take their time crossing the track.

Kelvin remembers having an argument with one of the ball boys. In fact, he had had a few arguments with ball boys and ground staff over the years but this was ridiculous. This discussion was not helped much by Dan Harding interjecting, *"I used to be one of them ball boys and that's what we were told to do. I was brilliant at it".* Thanks Dan.

Anyway, Kelvin says when the ball went behind the goal the ball boy at Brighton who was really *"a ball man"* would place it in the middle behind the goal so that Kelvin had to run round and get it. When the Saints took a 2-1 lead he started throwing the ball to Kelvin quicker and Kelvin simply laughed at him. *"Oh, you're speeding up a bit on the throw backs now".* He threw one back and Kelvin let it go past him just to show him what the frustration felt like.

The final memorable point about the game was the winning goal. As soon as the subject is mentioned Kelvin jumps in with *"You don't happen to remember who set that goal up?"* Yes, it was Kelvin who took a free kick wide near the touchline and his long ball was met by José Fonte at the back post who got on the score sheet with a strong header, despite David Connolly trying to get a nick on it on the line.

Kelvin recalls that the free kick was that wide that the Brighton manager Gus Poyet was standing only about a yard away. He had been critical about the Saints' style of play so Kelvin laughed inwardly because in the last minutes of such an important match there is only one place to put the ball and that is into the opposition's box. Kevin felt that any ball to the back post was going to be an opportunity. Kelvin can remember turning to look at Poyet but by the time he had turned the manager was back in the dugout and doing his best to avoid looking at Kelvin.

The goal set off crazy scenes as the visiting fans celebrated a goal that would surely see them promoted. The noise was almost deafening due in no small measure to José Fonte taking his shirt off in celebration. This set off many of the female fans who screamed as if One Direction had just walked in. Given his vantage point at the other end of the field Kelvin had not fully appreciated the mayhem in the crowd. Told of the reaction to José and his half-naked celebration Kelvin joked, *"Don't tell José – he might start growing his hair again".*

A special memory for one supporter that day was when Kelvin's mum, Lilian, ran and jumped on him at full time with a huge smile on her face, knowing the Saints had all but clinched promotion. His Mum and Dad constantly spare time to chat to fans and have come to share their passion, showing how much the club means to the Davis family.

....

And so the season moved towards its conclusion and in the following home game the Saints won 2-0 against Hartlepool whom Kelvin had played for briefly many years before. Now the Saints moved on to play Brentford away just one week after the excitement at Brighton.

As mentioned earlier Brentford was Geoff Davis's long-standing first club and here was Kelvin in a team that had to beat them to have a real chance of promotion. Kelvin says that he got little stick from his Dad when he played for Southampton at

Brentford. However, there were a couple of choruses from his Dad when he played for Sunderland against Brentford in an FA Cup match in January 2006. When Brentford went 2-1 up (the eventual final score) Kelvin recalls his Dad singing something like *"Kelvin Davis is a Brentford fan"*. But going there with Southampton for a game that the Saints needed to win for promotion was different for his Dad.

Essentially it was down to either the Saints or Huddersfield claiming automatic promotion to the Championship. The Saints were unbeaten in the previous 12 games, since 1 March when they had lost 1-0 at Walsall. Everyone connected with Southampton, both at the match and elsewhere, was looking out for the Huddersfield result and Kelvin recalls, *"We came off the pitch – I think we won 3-0 – and then we got the news that Huddersfield had won as well which meant that we were straight on the bus and down to Plymouth to try and achieve our goal down there".*

....

Venue: Home Park.
Opposition: Plymouth Argyle.
Date: Bank Holiday Monday, 2 May 2011.
Kick-off: 3.00 p.m.

Even the bare facts stir memories for all Saints fans. It was the only game that was being played that afternoon because the original fixture had been postponed. The Saints knew that a win would see them across the line bar some mathematical fluke on the following Saturday. Argyle knew that a defeat could take them down to League Two, so they would certainly put up a fight but try as they could and even with a late consolation goal the Saints won 3-1. The scenes in the visitors stand (and in other parts of the ground where Saints fans had got in with home fans) were extraordinary and heralded that the Saints were on the way back up.

Kelvin remembers it all vividly, including running from his goal at the far end of the pitch to reach the Saints' players and the supporters.

"I can remember it being a sunny day, the pitch was quite hard and firm and dry. I can remember the goals going in and I can remember the final score-line obviously. I can remember the final whistle going and we knew that the job was done. I don't know whether it was the joy of being promoted or the relief of getting across the line. It was the biggest feeling, the biggest emotion. I can remember getting up towards the other end and all the lads being there. I remember looking into the crowd and seeing my Mum and Dad and the guys that had made the trip up and, yeah, it was really emotional for those two reasons.

But the celebration that came after was – I'll just say it was such a fun great day especially travelling back on the bus. The bus drive home was absolutely fantastic. You didn't want the bus to stop. It was fantastic, a lot of singing. A bit of alcohol was consumed on the way back and it was, yeah, very special".

The alcohol continued to flow when the team got back to the bar after Plymouth. One minute Rickie Lambert was standing up perfectly alright and next minute he was flat on his back. As he hit the deck he split his eye open and so it was that he came to be bandaged up for the next game.

A more sober but nonetheless heartfelt reflection of the day appeared in the match day programme for the Walsall game the following week. In his Captains' Chat section Kelvin wrote:

"The perfectionist in me felt a tinge of disappointment as the clean sheet that would have capped the perfect day from a personal point of view was snatched away at the last…The secret to our success has been the inner belief and spirit that has proved crucial…We have a real sense of team unity here and it's not a case of the so-called star names like Rickie or Adam Lallana having a bigger billing than the rest in the dressing room…the gaffer [Nigel Adkins] has been working under tough circumstances from the off as promotion was all that was acceptable and he has done the job superbly".

He goes on to say that *"anything is possible"* and that the team would be looking for promotion in the next season.

Certainly the players knew how to enjoy themselves but, according to Kelvin, not all of them avoided the consequences of having a good time. After one night out Oscar Gobern was *"hanging".* At the team meeting the next day everyone was a little bit jovial –but there were some sore heads and Nigel Adkins started by saying, *"Well, obviously you've all had a night out. Did you all go together?" "Yes". "Okay, fair enough."*

Young Oscar was about 20 minutes late for the start of the meeting and the first barely audible words out of his mouth as he walked through the door were *"Good morning".* His voice sounded like gravel, a bit like Louis Armstrong, reducing everyone in the room to hysterical laughter.

....

The final Saints game at home was against Walsall who had surprisingly beaten the Saints a matter of weeks earlier at the Bescot stadium and had the potential to be party-poopers. The players and the fans might have expected it to fall a little flat after the scenes at Plymouth five days earlier but as Kelvin puts it, *"We were there to win a game of football and Nigel being the manager that he was, it was not finished until it was finished. It still turned out to be a fantastic day for me".*

The Saints won 3-1 but there was a strange moment towards the end of the game when the large contingency of Walsall fans began to celebrate and the home fans stared to join in with applause. Both sets of fans knew what was happening but on the pitch the Saints and Walsall players were confused because they did not know that other results were filtering through and that Walsall had been saved from the drop.

For Kelvin, *"The pitch invasion that followed was really a new experience for me so I really enjoyed it".* Perhaps the newest and the least enjoyable experience for Kelvin was being congratulated by an over-exuberant fan in his forties. Kelvin had certainly not been prepared for this man to kiss him full on and to try to "tongue him". He says the taste of stale beer and tobacco is still memorable when he thinks back to the incident.

After Plymouth the week before the celebrations were now more orchestrated as the players already knew what was planned for the evening. This was a period of time when there was a very close-knit group of *"wives, girlfriends, other halves and partners"* and Kelvin feels that this actually brought everyone together in the team and reinforced the reputation of Southampton being a family club. That night everyone went off to a hotel, had a meal and stayed over and *"it was a real nice togetherness feeling at the end of the season".*

....

The season 2011-12 is still fresh in the mind of Saints supporters, starting after what seemed a short summer and, following promotion from League One to the Championship, there was a positive feeling in the air but few believed in all honesty that there was another promotion in the offing.

Two games offer some interest in that season. Actually, one game that season was very, very special but let us take a look first at the match against Birmingham City at St Andrews on 4 February 2012.

It snowed heavily before, during and after the game and in the Hagiology publication *All the Saints* there is a fine picture of Morgan Schneiderlin brushing snow away with his hand in order to take a free-kick. Even some diehard Saints supporters expected the game to be called off but it was scheduled to be shown on television and therefore, it had to go ahead. The disgruntlement of the supporters that day is offset by a characteristically composed and professional view from Kelvin.

"I think there was pressure on the referee to play that game and we said once this game starts we've got to finish it. We didn't want to go through all of that again. I can remember making a save. It was one of them days when you make a save and you almost surprise yourself with it. That was against Marlon King. Right near the end of the game he hit a shot with his right foot and I remember I went full length. It was probably one of those where the weather gave me a bit of extra slide. I just caught it on the end of my fingertips, not being certain that I'd saved it. It could've so easily flashed inside the post but it didn't. Then you feel like you've contributed. We didn't want the game to go ahead and then lose".

The game finished 0-0.

The other game that lingers firmly in the memory for a few Saints fans (okay, every Saints fan) was also a televised match. It was an away game at Elland Road, Leeds, on 3 March 2012 and the Saints won 1-0.

In future record books the score line will read

Leeds United 0 Southampton 1

and will probably in itself attract little attention other than for supporters of Southampton. The Saints' goal was an excellent strike on 16 minutes by Rickie Lambert, so there was nothing remarkable in that. No, the remarkable thing was that the score stayed at 1-0 as a result of a performance of the highest quality by Kelvin in goal. Again and again he foiled attempts on goal by Leeds, including making one extraordinary double save. Anyone too young to remember it, especially any aspiring goalkeepers, should search for the video of the match on the internet.

The team was understandably ecstatic at the final whistle and could be seen mobbing Kelvin in his goal mouth. They were obviously pleased at getting three points and keeping a clean sheet. However, for one player, Dan Harding, it was more than that – it was personal and he owes his gratitude to Kelvin.

He explains why, *"I was on the bench for the game and then I came on after about 60 minutes. As a defender when you're winning 1-0 all you can do is fail really. If you concede a goal it looks like Dan Harding came on after 60 minutes and we conceded after 70.*

So the fact is that Kelvin had a fantastic game and we managed to keep a clean sheet. I was very thankful because I didn't want people looking at the game and thinking we only conceded when Mr Harding came on. Thankfully we did manage to keep a clean sheet. I remember one of the things was that to be promoted you need to have a little bit of everything. We had the quality and everything but without doubt you also need to have a bit of luck. You need to play in games where you think, how the hell did we win that? You need performances from certain individuals at certain times and that was Kelvin's time to win us the three points. Without that we might not have achieved what we wanted to achieve. Sometimes as a keeper you can have them type of games".

Dan, a close friend of Kelvin, was a former Leeds United player and he reminisces, *"I've had some really good results against Leeds every time I've played against them. I've scored against them twice and pretty much beaten them most times. I've always had good results against them. Obviously winning 1-0 was extra special for me as well".*

For Kelvin it was a *"perfect match"* and he can look back on it with great pleasure, even more so from the distance of time, *"As a sportsman, athlete or whatever it is, you're always striving to do better, always working every day to improve. You always think that perfection never comes because you're always striving for it but if I could pick a perfect day and a perfect game, Leeds away was probably the one. The one thing that really sticks in my head is a chance towards the end of the game. It was a bit of a goalmouth scramble, it was off the crossbar, making a block. Then the final whistle came very soon after and the fantastic feeling from my point of view is everyone was in the six-yard box at the time and as the whistle went there was a real embrace amongst the team. We kind of felt we'd achieved something special".*

The Leeds game did not in itself yield the promotion that Kelvin and the team yearned for but it certainly did help them on their way up to the Premier League for the 2012-13 season.

Saints fans will recall that there is an almost iconic photo of Kelvin clutching his Man-of-the-Match bottle of champagne, awarded by Sky Sports. It was an easy choice that day. In a characteristic gesture Kelvin gave the champagne to Jim Stannard, the Saints' first team goalkeeping coach at that time.

....

On 19 August 2012 Southampton played their first game back in the Premier League since 15 May 2005. Kelvin had spent a year less outside the top flight but the return was just as sweet nonetheless. However, after the way the team had worked so hard to get into the Premier League the Saints were dealt a very tough start. The opening run of games back in the top flight was away to Manchester City, at home to Wigan Athletic, at home to Manchester United and away to Arsenal.

The opening game was at the home of the champions and Kelvin and the others *"knew it was the toughest of tests away from home first game of the season".* Kelvin describes it as a *"poignant game"* in view of the team spirit that had been created and the togetherness of being promoted. Although they lost 3-2 the Saints had taken the lead to go 2-1 up. It was a goal by Rickie Lambert that gave them the lead and which he scored four minutes after coming off the bench.

Kelvin reflects on the fact that Rickie started the game on the bench. *"Probably a lot has been spoken of Rickie not starting a game which I think as a group of players – and without showing Nigel any disrespect – it surprised us. I think we felt that it wasn't right, that for everything he'd done, to not start that Premier League game. I spoke to him the night before and tried to ask him his feelings and just be positive with him I suppose and he just said* "Kelvin, I'm not going to let my not starting the game tomorrow ruin my Premier League experience. I've waited all my career for this." *And to be fair, that was his determination and everything he'd worked for to get to that level showed why he's gone on and achieved what he has".*

It is a notable sign of Kelvin's unselfishness that when he looks back on the game his prime concern is for Rickie Lambert and he does not immediately jump up and remind people that he saved a penalty from David Silva.

....

The second Premier League game was against Wigan Athletic at home but the excited anticipation of the supporters at being back in the top flight was cruelly dashed as the Saints lost 2-0. Then they lost 3-2 at home to Manchester United.

Next up was Arsenal away and Kelvin recalls losing the game 6-1. There were two own (or deflected) goals, one by Jos Hooiveld and the other one that went in off Nathaniel Clyne and slipped in at the near post. Kelvin further recollects that for either the first or second goal, *"it was Maya Yoshida's first or second game and he went kind of walkabout on a bit of defending and I got beat at the near post".*

But it was not the nature of the goals that made the impression on Kelvin. It was one of those days in football when a player can learn how ruthless the game can be, especially at the higher levels. The Saints were up against a strong Arsenal team at The Emirates so early in the season. *"They were very fresh and they took us to the cleaners if you like. Podolski's free kick was fantastic. I can remember after the game sitting in the dressing room and Nigel came in and said, "Well, I'm going to have to make changes" and the tone of how he said it was almost to me and I felt that he was … you could see … you could feel his immaturity of the Premier League. We'd spoken about it before the season started. For any team in the Premier League for the first time it's going to be like a rollercoaster and you can't afford to get too high or too low when you're in the Premier League. Especially when it's your first season because you can lose a game by 6 and then win the next week 1-0".*

Kelvin got the sense that, like the players, the manager too was learning at this level. Nigel Adkins said that he would need to make *"changes"* but Kelvin was sure there was only going to be one change in the forthcoming home game against Aston Villa and that would be him.

Professional pride made Kelvin feel that the manager had made the decision in haste when he chose to play Paulo Gazzaniga whom Kelvin felt was not ready. He is open in his view, *"I honestly felt that I was still the best man for the job at that time. It was a difficult time for me, not for not playing but because of the reasons for not playing".*

It was a tough time for Kelvin, made no better by the club signing Artur Boruc. Kelvin admits to being confused even though he was aware of the need for a squad to be as strong as possible in the Premier League. It was no criticism of Boruc but the club had only just signed Gazzaniga.

Kelvin was disappointed not only because he was not starting but also in the way that he found out about the change. He received a text message from a friend who had heard that Kelvin was not playing the next day. This was news to Kelvin but his friend had seen it somewhere on social media. So when he went in for training and

Nigel Adkins pulled him to one side and said he was going to play Gazza the next day Kelvin took the opportunity to say, *"Yeah, I was aware of that. I heard from social media that I wasn't playing."* The manager had told Paulo Gazzaniga the night before that he would be playing. Kelvin is full of praise for everything good that happened while Nigel Adkins was at the club but he admits simply that he *"felt let down at that point".*

Although Kelvin felt that he was not being given the respect he deserved he had no animosity towards Paulo who was just a young man coming to a Premier League club. Kelvin is perceptive enough to know that a manager might look at things differently but from a team perspective and in the dressing room Kelvin reveals that the players were *"confused with those decisions".*

....

Just after Christmas in the 2013-14 season the Saints played Everton at Goodison Park and lost 2-1. Despite an equaliser in the second half by Gaston Ramirez the match was effectively won in the first half. The Saints' supporters who were there that day will not know, until now, how one decision by Kelvin Davis affected the Saints' performance. Unusually, it was not a goalkeeping error that turned out to be the mistake that day. Kelvin was team captain for the match and now admits that, without thinking, he chose the wrong end to defend in the first half, which meant facing into the low, strong winter sunlight. He tried to find excuses and talk himself round with the players but he knew that they knew what he had done.

....

The opening game of the season at Manchester City in 2012-13 might have prompted some questions in the minds of Kelvin and others but fast forward to Manchester City in May 2015 and it was to be a happier venue for Kelvin. However, even that moment did not come without raising questions in his active mind.

Kelvin had passed the post-war record of goalkeeping appearances in goal for the Saints that was held by Eric Martin and had set his sights on reaching 300 appearances.

He achieved the record at Manchester City on the last day of the 2014-15 Premier League season but he had mixed feelings. Whilst achieving 300 appearances was a terrific honour he felt it was a shame that it did not come in front of a home crowd at St. Mary's when the Saints memorably beat Aston Villa 6-1.

Kelvin had thought he might achieve the milestone in the away game at Leicester City but the manager explained that he had decided to give Paulo two games and have an opportunity to see him play. It was a difficult pill to swallow but as expected Kelvin dealt with it in his highly professional way. However, when told that he was going to play in the last game of the season because of the milestone he found his mind in turmoil.

As Kelvin explains, *"I've always been the sort of character that I didn't want anything unless I'd deserved it and I felt that maybe he was giving me that appearance because it was the milestone rather than warranted in terms of my ability. But I think, looking back on the game, I proved that it was my ability that made the saves in that game. Although we obviously didn't get anything from that game, from my contribution I did all that I could have done".*

Anyone close to Kelvin will confirm that he does not particularly like contrived celebrations and, by his own admission, he was less than inclined to celebrate because he was disappointed with the result, the Saints having lost 2-0. However, he had managed to ensure that at least his two older children were able to get to the game. Kelly could not be at the match as she had to stay at home to look after their very young son, added to which, there was an evening do in Southampton and it would have been impossible for Kelly to get back in time. However, it was important to him to have his two older children there, as well as his Mum and Dad and his best friend Rooty and his family. Kelvin reflects on his reaction, *"I've seen a picture of me blowing a kiss … that wasn't really to anyone in particular and I don't really know why I did it. I don't think I've ever kissed a badge. I have no problem with kissing the Saints badge but it's just something that's never been in my make-up to do. It was a special moment, it was kind of a "thank you" really. That 300 had come round so quick and yet so slow".*

As the much-loved and highly-respected elder statesman in the Southampton ranks, Kelvin is looked up to by all of the players and it was no surprise that in the few days following the Manchester City match, a number of players, as well as family members, were eager to pass on their messages of congratulations to the popular club captain.

Kelvin is clearly credited by a number of ex-colleagues as an ambassador for the dressing room and for the club as a whole, while the landmark figure of appearances was also heralded as something to treasure.

In no particular order, the following are the fulsome tributes to Kelvin from team mates, past and present, which appeared on the Saints website in the days following his 300th appearance.

José Fonte:

"I think that people like him are the most important in the dressing room. He's a leader, he's an example as a professional. He's a big character and he's a clown as well – he makes people laugh. Especially for the kids he is one they need to look up to because he's a great professional and a great example how to conduct yourself and be a good football player."

We've been on a great journey. I could say on numerous occasions where we shared some great memories. It's well documented that we've been all through the leagues. It's just fantastic what he, and we, were able to achieve together and he was massive for us throughout all those years.

When we have a meal on an away game once in a while we share some moments and thoughts about what we accomplished and what we achieved. It's always great to remember but time doesn't stop, you have to keep moving forward and keep trying to create more memories and greater achievements."

José expressed the hope that he too can reach 300 games for the club, "I told him I'm going to catch him! I want to go as far as I can. I just need to keep fit and healthy and try to be selected every week."

Chris Perry:

"To do it at one club certainly, and for the longevity of him as well to have played in League 1 and still be doing as well as he has done in the Premier League is testament to just how good a keeper he is.

He's a superb professional. Kelvin is the first out on the training pitches every single morning and he's the last one off it too. He's so full of enthusiasm around the place, he's a fantastic professional and the reason he's still playing at the level he is, at his age in the first team over the past few games is down to that. It's a testament to his dedication, not only to his own game, but to the love of the football club as well.

He loves Southampton and being down there which is something you can really see in every day during training."

Jos Hooiveld:

"Kelv for me is the representation of Southampton F.C. After the first training session I knew the standards of how the boys talked both to and with each other and what the club stood for. He organised all the nights out and the only negative was that it was always my card that had to be put down as a deposit! I will never forget the barbeque at his place and the outfit he wore, he pulled it off though."

Danny Butterfield:

"Kelvin has always been the gaffer in the dressing room. His commitment and drive to be a success as a person passes on to his team mates and has driven Southampton forward from that dressing room over the years. I've shared unbelievable memories with Kelv and probably at the expense of others.

He can switch on the practical jokes and be back as SKD ready to train with fire in his belly within minutes. Most importantly, a true friend and gent who I miss seeing in my dressing room every day."

Lee Barnard:

"SKD is a top keeper, top professional and a top man. One of the nicest guys in football and a massive influence on the whole dressing room. All keepers are a bit mad, and Kelv is no exception. I'm not surprised at all Kelv has been at the top for such a long time, one of the best keepers I've played with. Congrats mate."

Richard Chaplow:

"Congratulations on reaching such a milestone. I'd like to say here's to another 300 but I think that may even be out the reach of SKD. Nothing but fond memories of Kelv, on and off the pitch. A fantastic player, and great leader, but more importantly a top guy. Keep up the good work, love Chappy (your favourite baldy)."

Paul Wotton:

"99% of my memories of me and Kelv are unprintable so I'll go boring: best keeper I've played with by a mile, great professional and great friend! Congratulations big boy!!!"

Drew Surman:

"Kelv was my roomy for a couple of years at Southampton. I was only young at the time but he was always full of good advice on and off the pitch which has helped me massively in my career. He's a true professional and leader, and I've got to say he's one of the funniest guys I've had the pleasure of playing with!! Well done Super!"

Jason Puncheon:

"He was a leader to many young players coming through at a big club at a young age...he led by example in training every day. I will never forget his performance away at Leeds in the Championship - the best goalkeeping performance I have seen and been a part of. Great credit to reach so many games at a great club!!"

Dan Harding:

"I have the utmost respect for Kelvin Davis! He was a huge influence on me during my time at Southampton and the rock that got us back to back promotion. He is a complete comic while always remaining professional and the best captain I have worked with. I feel very lucky to have played with him and been captained by him and even luckier to say he is a great friend!! He's completely dedicated to Southampton and I wouldn't be surprised to see him manage them one day!"

Rickie Lambert:

"Super Kelvin Davis!!! I had five incredible years with Saints and Kelv had as big an influence on me as much as anyone. His personality and professionalism stood out straightaway, but he also knew how to let his hair down on the right occasion, which is probably why we became so close!! He's a top 'keeper, and a top bloke, and I'm proud to say that I played alongside him for as long as I did. 300 games is a great achievement and I wish him and Saints even more success in the future."

Lee Holmes:

"Kelvin Davis is someone that I will always look up to, literally, and he's the best keeper that I've had the pleasure of playing with. He was the number one joker around the dressing room, but when it was time to work there was no-one more professional than Kelvin.

I'm proud to have played with you, and even more proud to have you as a best friend."

Jack Cork:

"Well done Super! Can't believe you are still going. Actually, I can with the amount of extra work you always put in. Great player and even better person, especially behind closed doors!

I'll never forget Leeds away in the season we went up."

Mum and Dad:

"We are so proud of what you have achieved. Well done, son. We know how much this football club means to you."

Dean Hammond:

"Congratulations to Kelvin on his 300th appearance. A fantastic achievement. He is one of the best professionals I have worked with, has always been so dedicated and driven to success which has influenced my career. The life and soul of the dressing room and a pleasure to play alongside.

One of my best memories will always be lifting the trophy with him at Wembley. Top man."

Kelly, Emelia, Sonnie and Buddy:

"Well, Kel, since you've been 17 you've always had goals and something to work towards, but if someone told you when we arrived in Southampton that you'd reach the big 300, then I think you'd have found it hard to believe. You did it, and myself, Emelia, Sonnie & Buddy (he doesn't know it yet but he will when he's older) are ridiculously proud of you. You deserve every little bit of credit you are given for this achievement. I'm now intrigued to hear your next milestone… more games I expect!

Love and congratulations…"

Maya Yoshida:

"When someone comes into the club for the first time, he finds things out for you, and it's why the club is so welcoming. I think Kelv is one of the greatest people I know as a player, but also as a character he is friendly and professional. Even though he has been here a long time and with Boruc or Fraser playing here, he is always positive and good for the club.

The first time you go away with the team you have to sing a song in front of the lads and he is always leading that by tapping the glasses on the table."

"I'm very, very happy to see him reach his 300th appearance for Southampton because I think he'll be here for the rest of his life," said the Japanese international.

"He's a funny guy too, but I can't tell you any of the stories that he is behind!"

....

In light of Maya Yoshida mentioning how funny Kelvin can be there are examples of what Rickie Lambert and others call his *"ruthless"* sense of humour but possibly the best example is that of 'secret Santas'.

The practice of giving secret Santas gradually grew in status after Kelvin had started it off when the club were in their first season in League One. The presents were never supposed to be particularly nice and team mate and co-conspirator Paul Wotton admits that many of the gifts were "too disgusting" to be described in print. But the more humiliating and upsetting a present was, the more fun it meant for everybody as they revelled in the embarrassment of the recipient. Of course, nobody knew who had chosen the particular gift which avoided there being resentment against a single team mate.

Kelvin reckons that the secret Santa is now an established tradition that is done every year and he admits, *"Maya Yoshida's an easy target because the lads just get him everything that's Chinese just to wind him up".*

When Jack Cork was at the club, Kelvin recalls that as soon as it got to December Corky would be pestering him, *"When are we going to do secret Santa?"* There is a rule that if someone gets a gift of an item of clothing then they have to wear it for first part of the warm-up at training. Imagine Steven Davis in a nun's outfit or Jordy Clasie in a baby outfit. Some of the clothing gifts go close to the bone but Kelvin says they *"remain in the dressing room",* although there are photos. Perhaps one day...

Kelvin himself lists the secret Santa gifts that he has received: a Zimmer frame, a dirty old man's costume, a shirt with 'Southampton's Number Four' written on the back and a retirement book which he says was *"very nice".* Some players might not have fully understood the concept and there were ordinary gifts like tooth paste, toothbrush, mouthwash and the types of thing that set *"the mind thinking".*

....

Notwithstanding the celebration of the 300th appearance of Kelvin in goal, 2014-15 had not quite reached its conclusion for Southampton. Supporters and everyone associated with the club watched avidly for the result of the FA Cup Final to learn whether they would be going into the Europa League. Arsenal duly won the FA Cup and in July 2015 the Saints would be playing in the Europa League – its first venture into Europe since 2003.

It was highly appropriate for the views of the influential and popular club captain to be reported with Kelvin saying that qualification for the Europa League is the natural next step for Southampton. He found he could use only one word to express his emotions, *"To sum it up in one word is 'proud'. The feeling of finishing seventh and being in a European competition – the only word I can use is 'proud'. I'm proud of my teammates, proud of the club and proud of what everyone has achieved. To be a club like Southampton and progress as we have done, to me it's the natural next step to qualify for European competition.*

We've progressed year on year and for us to finish seventh in the Premier League ahead of so many fantastic football clubs to put ourselves in this position warranted the opportunity to play in Europe.

We needed Arsenal to win the cup but at the same time that position of seventh is what has given us the opportunity. We're very excited and looking forward to the prospect of playing in the Europa League next year. But we've still got a hurdle to come across (the third qualifying round) and that's what we'll be focusing on".

"I think it's about going into the competition with your eyes open", he added. *"We know we're still growing. We've got a group of players that want to keep improving. We won't shy away from the challenge. We're fortunate we've got a manager who has European football experience."*

The Saints would join the competition at the third qualifying round stage at the end of July 2015 and Kelvin was convinced that it would not faze the squad.

"The lads will be more than happy to be in and amongst it preparing for one of the biggest seasons in the club's history."

Goalkeepers and Goalkeeping

The key question about any footballer is the degree to which talent is so exceptional that it necessitates no hard work or can hard work make up for shortfalls in talent?

The question is clearly irrelevant in the case of Kelvin Davis in that he has great natural talent which combines with his propensity for sheer hard work. The combination of the two is what has made Kelvin the goalkeeper he is.

Kelvin's is not the type of character that gets star-struck or in awe of anyone. As he sees it, *"We all go to bed at night, shut our eyes, go to sleep and when we're there on our own we're all pretty similar people and similar make up".* However, he has to admit that his childhood goalkeeping hero was the former Saint Peter Shilton. He cannot deny it because his Mum Lilian confirms it as being true.

However, as a youngster he was still not sure that he was going to be a goalkeeper so his respect for Shilton was about what he had achieved, even more so knowing that Shilton was still playing for England at 40 years of age.

Becoming a goalkeeper did not seem to be his first choice when he played in his school football team where all the boys had to play in different positions. Kelvin played in midfield and up front as well as in goal. His former PE teacher, Sean Downey recalls that he would always move Kelvin up front when the team needed a goal and Kelvin would almost always come up with one.

His close school friend is Steve Root ('Rooty') who also saw himself as a goalkeeper. He recalls watching from the side lines when the school was playing in a semi-final of the County Cup. The weather was *"vile"* and Kelvin's school was playing downhill with the wind behind them in the first half. They managed to reach half-time with a 1-0 lead.

In the second half one of the opposition put in a high and dipping shot which the wind was taking and, according to Rooty, was a *"certain goal"* that would have put the score at 1-1. However, to everyone's surprise Kelvin made a fantastic save and tipped the ball over the bar. As good as that was for Kelvin it gave Rooty a real sinking feeling because he knew that his chance to become the school's goalkeeper had disappeared in the face of the natural talent of his school mate.

....

Rooty saw all this in his best mate Kelvin as well as his dedication and commitment that shone through both in and out of school in 1993.

Kelvin Davis: *Report from Year 11, 1993*

Provided by **Mr Downey (Head of Icknield House and PE Teacher)**

Kelvin is a confident, articulate and every personable student, who is extremely popular with both staff and his peers. He is making good progress in most of his subjects, particularly in PE where he excels. It is refreshing to note Kelvin's commitment to attending 'extra PE lessons' - unfortunately his German and General Studies teachers are less pleased; it is usually at the expense of those lessons!

Kelvin has represented the school, district and county with distinction at football and has every chance of making it as a professional footballer now he recognises that he is a goalkeeper not a centre-forward! Nevertheless, in crucial games he has 'thrown off the gloves' and used his height and aggression (and he constantly reminds me, 'skill') to create and score vital goals in the school's county and national trophy successes.

Above all, Kelvin is an outstanding leader and communicator, inspiring others to greater feats through demonstrating his own commitment and dedication. A fearless young man with all the attributes to become a successful professional sportsman. We will miss him but our loss will be Luton Town's gain.

As well as having a natural talent Kelvin didn't leave it at that and his friend Rooty recalls how his dedication and strong self-discipline showed itself from a young age.

"Kel, Kel come on mate just have a beer, you won't get on, Pleat won't play a 17 year old goalkeeper". Just as a best mate should at the age of 17, Rooty was trying to tempt his pal to down a couple of cans to start the weekend.

"No mate", he said, *"you know I can't, I couldn't live with myself, I've worked so hard over the last three years to get this close to the first team. I am ready".*

Ten minutes later the phone call came and sure enough Super KD's career opener was set for Luton Town FC under David Pleat away at Stoke City. Rooty cannot remember the game but says he remembers the night before *"like it was just yesterday".*

As he went through his career Kelvin admired and respected goalkeepers not so much because they were blessed with heights of 6'4" or taller, but those who, without the luxury of size and height, had to work very hard on their technique. The work ethic consistently comes through from Kelvin. Kelvin always felt that there was no point in modelling himself on other goalkeepers. To compare himself with someone like David Seaman was pointless because he was tall at 6'4" and had a different stature. As Kelvin remarks, *"I saw someone like Antti Niemi making saves week in week out in the Premier League and he's not 6'6'"".* In what he calls his *"Southampton era"* Kelvin admired and respected the likes of Shay Given and Brad Friedel who were still performing at such a high level, as well as Jussi Jääskeläinen who was playing *"ridiculously well"* at West Ham United at the time.

....

When Kelvin joined Southampton he was approaching the age of 30 which got him thinking ahead about being able to keep going. He had back issues at Ipswich and had done a lot of yoga in an attempt to keep flexible and mobile. One of the constants for Kelvin in his ten seasons at Southampton is the assistance and expertise he has had from the physiotherapists.

The first person he met in the physiotherapy department was Andy Barr who had just come to the club and with whom Kelvin was at school. Andy was head of sports medicine at Southampton and had experienced a season as injury prevention specialist for Manchester City, as well as seven years with Bolton Wanderers, including one season as head of First Team physiotherapy. In 2009 he went to basketball team New York Knicks and was promoted to Director, Conditioning and Fitness after the 2012-13 season.

Andy has developed an expertise in movement style and using video recording as a way of feeding back to athletes in any field. The days of using a bit of ultrasound or another piece of equipment to improve fitness and performance have long since passed. Physiotherapy is nearly all about working with an individual's movement.

Fortunately, Matt Radcliffe, who trained with Andy Barr, was also a movement specialist. Being something of a workaholic, Matt would put in all the hours needed, including home visits, to support players and to ensure that they made the speediest recovery possible. When he had his back injury, Kelvin became very close to Matt, finding that he left no stone unturned in order to make good progress with Kelvin's recovery.

Kelvin continues to have nothing but admiration and respect for all the physiotherapists and sports scientists at the club. One of the current senior physiotherapists, Tom Sturdy, learned a great deal from Matt Radcliffe and Kelvin now works with Tom with any issues that require attention.

As he got into his mid-thirties Kelvin was looking at what other goalkeepers were still achieving and he started to think about how to prolong his career. He had worked for a long time with the physiotherapists at the club including Emma Gimpel and Suzanne Scott.

Emma has known Kelvin since he first came to the club. She had been there herself since 2004 and when he joined she was in the process of becoming full-time. Emma immediately recognised his qualities, *"He was a massive personality from day one. He is a natural leader and a true professional in the way that he approaches everything – training, the way he looks after himself and his body".*

Emma was involved in Kelvin's general rehab and prehab. She has a special interest in Pilates, movement therapy and movement re-training and that cemented their special working relationship.

Kelvin would go to Emma every morning to do an hour of Pilates before training. She says, *"He actually became fantastic at doing it and I strongly believe that it has enabled him to play at the level he has for so long. It staved off some back injuries that had been hovering around in the background for a number of years. He really felt the benefit of it".*

Emma echoes what other people say about him in that he *"was one of the players who really went above and beyond and went the extra mile. When he did training he always made sure he did extra".* Emma is convinced that he did what it takes to remain Number One because he never failed to look after himself.

Although the physio sessions were always built on hard work Emma still fell victim, like so many other people, to his sense of humour. *"He would have me in stitches every day. I would laugh at the craziness that he used to get up to".* Apart from his crazy sense of humour she says that he is an inspiration to be around and she now classes him as a friend as well as a work colleague.

Later in the book Malcolm Webster will talk about the work that Kelvin had to do on his glutes. Emma confirms this and they worked together on his hamstring and his glutes. The focus for Emma was on his functional training, in other words what he needed in order to do his job as a goalkeeper. That meant *"doing a lot of work on his glutes, on power, on mobility, on motor patterning and the way his muscles fire up and in what order – to try and optimise his power and his range".*

Together Emma and Suzanne worked closely with Kelvin and as Emma points out they were *"doing stuff with him that I believe wasn't widely done"* although you see a lot more of it now than ten years ago. The club really pioneered prehab, which means working out where someone's body might fail before it failed and then putting in place a programme to address it. As Emma says, *"He was the master at it, he was the master. He is probably still the master at the club and I believe he's really felt the benefit of it within his game".*

Emma's colleague Suzanne has a background in dance skills that are important to body movement, especially the upper body movement that is particularly important for goalkeepers and for their capacity to change position in a matter of a split second.

Kelvin was sceptical about Pilates at first but he saw it made sense and now he is glowing with praise, finding that it has been highly effective, *"I started doing a couple of sessions a week and I felt that really improved my flexibility in terms of keeping my mobility. I progressed in terms of my age. It really supported me on the pitch and obviously with Suzanne having the knowledge she's got, even to this day with the aches and pains you get with being 39 and training every day, she's got healing hands and she's very much one of the reasons why I'm still able to perform at this level".*

Talking to the physiotherapists it is clear that Kelvin has a range of qualities that serve him so well as a goalkeeper. He has a very high capacity to focus, but if he has to shift focus he can invariably pick up where he left off. His instinct is to get to the heart of a movement exercise because he is very exact and likes to strip things back.

Pilates is also very good for concentration and the ability to be able to process several things at once. Given his ability to do this Suzanne has nicknamed him *"split screen man".*

For the physiotherapy department he is intelligent, fit, robust, a natural leader, a razor sharp sense of humour and warm and compassionate. He has a blend of supreme confidence and modesty and he will succeed in whatever he chooses to do in the future.

....

Physiotherapy and hard work on his fitness may have held Kelvin in good stead but behind every good goalkeeper is a good coach. Kelvin has been privileged to work with a series of excellent coaches who, with their different approaches to training, have enabled him to broaden his skills in different ways.

Foremost among the coaches he has worked with is his *"coach and mentor"* Malcolm Webster who Kelvin first knew at Luton Town when he was only 19 or 20.

In those days at Luton Town there was no full-time goalkeeping coach but the part-time coach was Peter 'the Cat' Bonetti. Best known for his Chelsea and England careers, Peter was by then in his fifties. Then Luton signed a goalkeeper called Fred Barber who, according to Kelvin *"opened my eyes a little bit as to how mad some goalkeepers can be".* Fred was quite a character and used to go out wearing a mask before games. He had hit the headlines in May 1992 when he wore his mask as he walked out with the teams at Wembley stadium, playing for Peterborough United in the Division 3 play-off final against Stockport County. United won 2-1.

Fred took Kelvin under his wing and said, *"You've got to come and work with this coach called Malcolm Webster. He lives over Cambridge way and I'll take you over one day".* And so Kelvin found himself in a college field, training with someone he had never met before. He still remembers the first session with Malcolm which was *"very, very intense".* They did a lot of up and down work, a lot of cone work and goalkeeper specific training.

What sticks out in Kelvin's memory is the recovery time. *"Malcolm used to let you just walk across the box, come back and then you'd start again".* This was an eye-opener in terms of what a goalkeeper can do and how hard you can work, even as a person as well. Kelvin can remember for the first time feeling *"jelly legs and a bit sick during the training session".* This approach might be called *"old school"* now but for Kelvin it put him on the start of a great learning curve. Kelvin looks back and knows, *"that was Malcolm's way of seeing what I was made of and seeing what type of character you are and how hard you want to work".*

Fred spoke to the manager and this resulted in Malcolm coming in for two sessions a week. He combined this with coaching Richard Wright at Ipswich and Kevin Miller who was at Crystal Palace. There is no doubting the huge significance of being coached by Malcolm Webster who *"did wonders for my early career in terms of coaching those principles that I still abide by today".*

Kelvin then spent four years at Wimbledon where he worked with Stuart Murdoch who would eventually take on a role at Southampton under Alan Pardew. When Wimbledon went into administration Kelvin had a couple of opportunities, one of which was Ipswich Town where Joe Royle was the manager and where Malcolm Webster was now working full-time.

That made the decision to go to Ipswich easy for Kelvin and, although he was under no illusions, he liked to think that Malcolm had told Joe Royle good things about him. He went there but only worked with Malcolm for one season because George Burley got the manager's job at Derby and Malcolm went to work with George. They were their own team and when they eventually went to Southampton it was as a package.

Kelvin went from Ipswich to Sunderland and after a stint at Hearts George Burley and Malcolm Webster arrived at Southampton. The rest is history, as they say, and Kelvin simply had to sign for the Saints when the offer was made. Apart from feeling very at home from his first day at Southampton, Kelvin is clear that Malcolm being at the club was *"a massive reason for me to sign".*

....

Given that Kelvin has a natural propensity for hard work, he easily took to the way Malcolm worked. Every coaching session with Malcolm was well thought out but otherwise quite simple. He had a strategy and he always worked with cones and usually it would be a four cone square. That might not mean much to anyone who is not a goalkeeper but in goalkeeping terms it means mostly defending a four-yard goal ensuring your angles are right. Working with Malcolm always meant working continuously with cones and a four-yard goal.

Malcolm had rules that any goalkeeper who has worked with him will find familiar. Kelvin recalls one such rule, *"If you knock a cone over you start again – regardless".* As soon as he knocked over a cone Kelvin would breathe a deep sigh of, *"I've got to go again now".* For Kelvin *"training with Malcolm was always about short sharp bursts of work which made you feel physically fit and very strong. Working when you are tired has a bonus in that it creates a mental strength because you have to keep going. Malcolm was always prepared to do extra with a 'keeper. In fact, he always wanted to do more. If he was running an afternoon session for the younger 'keepers the more senior 'keepers were always welcome to join that session".*

What Malcolm imbued most in Kelvin was hard work and the emphasis on being professional. In football in those days, not so much now, Sundays and Wednesdays were days off. That was the pattern of the week but Malcolm had the attitude that *"you work for your days off".* Kelvin is clear, *"Subsequently it gave me a fantastic foundation".*

When George Burley moved on, Malcolm remained working with the squad under Nigel Pearson up to the end of the season. But when the new season started with Jan Poortvliet and Mark Wotte, Malcolm did not wholly agree with things that were happening at the club. It got to the stage where it was affecting him at work and away from work, so he and the club took the decision that his services were no longer needed. Kelvin says that, although there is no substantial evidence, the feeling was that anyone with any experience was being moved aside.

Kelvin still has *"utmost respect"* for Malcolm and he has no doubt that other 'keepers who have worked with him (such as Andy Marshall and Lee Camp) would all express the same sentiment.

....

Kelvin first encountered Keith Granger when Malcolm Webster would bring him in to watch, observe and occasionally to take a session. Kelvin and Keith instantly hit it off because they were of like mind in terms of trying to search every avenue for ways to improve.

Keith came in to help out when Jan Poortvliet was manager. Alongside working at the docks Keith was training the under 21s and Kelvin had worked with him on a part-time basis in the past. They had built up a good relationship with the earlier sessions, became very close and with him being local, Keith is someone who Kelvin can still rely on.

All smiles at Hillsborough, Sept 2010

At former club Ipswich, Aug 2011
Saints won 5-2

*A love-in at Leeds
(courtesy of Daily Echo)*

*Man of the Match at Leeds
(courtesy of Daily Echo)*

Scorer and Saver at Leeds

Anything my Dad can do …

If in doubt,
always wear red

A top class take at Cardiff, Sept 2011

Promotion crowd, May 2011

My family at St Mary's

This is my Daddy

Emelia and Sonnie at the JPT Final

I think I might go into films!

A happy man

saintstv.com

Carlsberg T··Mobile·

flybe.com flybe.com

T··M Carlsberg

flybe.com

The BB era (Before Beards)

Your ear is cold young Josh

Let's start this promotion party

We are going up! We are going up!

Loving Father

*Proud family man
(with two heads!)*

*Davis Senior focused on the game
while Mum has a laugh*

Promotion party, May 2011

I'd love to play down there

You're supposed to be in goal!

He's behind you

Back in the Premier League Man City, Aug 2012

Stretching – the Pilates paid off

Saints vs Leicester City, 17 October 2015, Premier League

Keith offered to *"help out wherever I can"*. With the sort of character that Keith is that meant from 7 o'clock in the morning until 7 o'clock the next morning. Keith had a passion for goalkeeping and for life itself and was thrilled to be working for Southampton and bringing a direct influence to the club. He and Kelvin would do three sessions a day on some days. Keith has two sons – Billy and James. Billy is a goalkeeper and he was in the academy at the time. On occasions Keith and Kelvin would work with him.

Kelvin was at the training ground one Monday morning and he had won the Player of the Month trophy. He thinks it was the Monday of the third or fourth month in succession. It was at the old training ground and Kelvin had parked his car round the back. As was invariably the case Kelvin was one of the first players to arrive but he declines to say whether this was because of sheer enthusiasm or in order to get the best parking spot, *"up the top"*.

His car was easy to find and Kelvin despatched Billy Granger to collect something from the boot of his car which Keith thought was risky because all Kelvin's gloves could have gone missing. He handed Keith a cardboard box and said, *"That's for you"*. He opened it and saw it was the trophy for Player of the Month and he said, *"Well done mate. That's brilliant. You really deserve that.* He said, *"No, no, that's for you. I couldn't have done it without you"*. Not often lost for words Keith admits that on this occasion, *"I couldn't think of what to say"*, adding with a touch of emotion, *"I could really respect him being so appreciative of me and I've got that feeling now. It's still nice and shiny and in my house now"*.

Kelvin is quick to acknowledge that Keith had a massive hand in terms of his progression and pushing on to the next level. It was not just for the sessions he put on but for everything. He would look at a player from all different angles, not just in terms of what was happening on the pitch and the training ground. He believed that a player should seek how to improve or organise his private life so as to be able to give more time to work on your goalkeeping.

Keith had some fantastic ideas and was always thinking outside the box, even indoor training. Kelvin remembers undertaking a rebound session in the dome, off the brick wall, moving round and landing on crash mats.

Keith was the first coach who Kelvin worked with who used to take video recordings of their sessions. Every two or three weeks he used to make up a fresh DVD of Kelvin's distribution and saves. Kelvin says he was quite inventive and even put music to it. One of the first DVDs that he made for Kelvin was called *"Inches to Performance"*. *"No pun intended"*, claims Kelvin with a smile, adding that *"it was my first experience where that was done by him personally for me. It makes you realise how well you're doing".*

Keith had been working part-time for the club throughout all of Kelvin's time there but their strong working relationship was curtailed with the arrival of a new manager, although they have remained great friends ever since. Alan Pardew and Keith did not quite hit it off and he brought in Stuart Murdoch.

Characteristically, Kelvin respected the decision of the new manager who pulled Kelvin to one side and said, *"I'm going to bring in my own man. It's not to the detriment of Keith or what Keith's doing. It's just that I want to put my own stamp on it".* In any job, any manager would want to do that and to retain a working relationship with his *"own man".*

....

Kelvin had worked with Stuart Murdoch as a coach before and so he arrived as a friendly face. Kelvin had always respected him for his openness and honesty, two adjectives that apply equally to Kelvin. Kelvin and Stuart developed a good working relationship.

For some time, there was an overlap when both Keith and Stuart were working at the club. Stuart would come in and observe the session that Kelvin was doing with Keith, and allowed things that they did, and the ways they trained, to continue. He was very professional and never ever showed any animosity towards Keith. He seemed happy for Kelvin to continue with whatever he wanted so long as the performances were there on the pitch. He even replicated some of what Keith had done alongside his own ideas and ways of working. He would also put on the types of sessions that Keith had done because he knew that Kelvin felt the benefit. Keith took it as a compliment that someone would continue his work.

If Stuart was unaware then, he will be made aware now that Keith and Kelvin were meeting at the park on certain days when Kelvin felt he needed an additional session. Kelvin says that it wasn't exactly matter of cleaning away dog mess before they started diving around but it was not too far off it. He continues with a grin, *"It was the love of the game and the love of diving around".* They did get recognised a couple of times but they *"always managed to get away with it".*

....

Toni Jiménez was part of the team that came to the club with Mauricio Pochettino, along with Jesus Pérez and Miguel D'Agostino. They worked in a slightly different way in that they were a very close-knit team. Toni is a passionate person by nature, particularly about goalkeeping and goalkeepers. He has very strong beliefs on what he likes and expects from a goalkeeper.

Mauricio believes the most important person in the team is the goalkeeper and coming from a manager that was a breath of fresh air for Kelvin. The belief was that the goalkeeper is the last line of defence but also the first line of attack. So, a lot of emphasis was put on goalkeeper training. There was a great deal of work on playing out from the back and training in a pattern of play into the goalkeeper. Toni's style of goalkeeping was very outfield-minded and this was reflected in that there was a lot of training with your feet. He was the first goalkeeping coach Kelvin had where 50% of the training was about distribution. But the style of play that Mauricio was trying to encourage in matches justified why Kelvin and the others trained so hard on that aspect of their game.

As well as being very passionate Toni is also very proud and his love of goalkeeping could be felt throughout the training. After a session Kelvin says that he would always look for your feedback, such as *"what your feelings were, how could we improve, how could that session be better, did you feel there was enough time?"* Toni was very highly focused and when Kelvin went into his office to see him he would find that he had video clip after video clip of just one save. They were the first team of coaches that were technically minded with two cameras just homed in on the goalkeeper at any one time during training. How feedback has changed since the time that David Pleat tapped the young Kelvin on the shoulder at half-time.

Kelvin was very positive about the feedback knowing that it was all part of continuous improvement. Some people might feel uncomfortable being under constant observation with the numbers of cameras on them, but Kelvin felt that it was a great way to learn. If he had done something in training and found himself asking, *"How did I make that save?"* or, *"I didn't make that save, I wonder why?"* it was always there to refer back to. That was the eye-opener, the innovation from Toni and the team.

Kelvin found that during this period it was probably the most that he had trained with the outfield team. Toni and the team had a philosophy that *"everyone comes out together, everyone stays together".* The goalkeepers used to break off to do their warm-up, the team breaks off to do their warm-up and then after 20-25 minutes all the players came back together to perform the drills that Mauricio and the team put on for them.

In contrast the present coach, Dave Watson, has an approach which entails the 'keepers going out some 45 minutes before the team, getting all their work done, including technical training and fitness work. Then they join in with the team when they come out.

Dave Watson believes that you can get more training that is specific to goalkeepers when you are away from the team. Kelvin does not deny that is true – it is simply different to how Toni and Mauricio worked as Toni used to do specific goalkeeping work at the end of the session.

Achievements

Facts and numbers by themselves can never fully reflect the qualities of someone as both a footballer and as a man.

Throughout the time spent compiling this book Kelvin has insisted that he did not want his celebration book to be *"boring"*. So, with apologies to him, here is his record as a Saint followed by a match by match record.

In his ten seasons Kelvin has played in **301** matches of which **203** were either won or drawn. This means that two-thirds of the games he played in ended in positive results.

The numbers of goals conceded in those **301** games was **366**, whereas **472** goals were scored for the Saints. Kelvin has kept **95 clean sheets** in his time at Southampton. In his Club Captain's notes for the Saints vs West Ham match day magazine on 6 February 2016 Kelvin acknowledges that *"clean sheets are not just down to the goalkeeper".* He goes on to say that it is the collective effort of the team that produces such positive results.

Kelvin has won a number of personal awards and accolades during his time as a Saint, including:

- **League One Team of the Year** 2009-10

- **League One Team of the Year** 2010-11

- **Championship Team of the Year** 2011-12

- **Championship Team of the Week** – on several occasions
  and especially in March 2012 following his performance at Leeds

- **Away Player of the Season** awarded by the Saints Travel Club:
  2008-09 and 2009-10

- the **Lev Yashin** shirt awarded by Sky Sports Soccer AM
  to a 'keeper who has kept three consecutive clean sheets.

Kelvin has played against 72 clubs in the various football leagues and in one case a non-league club in the FA Cup which happened to be the first club he played for, Luton Town. He has faced three clubs more often than any others, playing nine times against each of the following: Barnsley, Burnley and Ipswich Town. The following lists the clubs which Kelvin has played against, on the number of occasions shown.

ARSENAL	1	MIDDLESBROUGH	2
BARNSLEY	9	MILLWALL	5
BIRMINGHAM CITY	6	MK DONS	6
BLACKPOOL	4	NORTHAMPTON TOWN	1
BOLTON WANDERERS	1	NORWICH CITY	7
BOURNEMOUTH	3	NOTTINGHAM FOREST	4
BRENTFORD	4	NOTTS COUNTY	3
BRIGHTON & HOVE ALBION	6	OLDHAM ATHLETIC	4
BRISTOL CITY	6	PETERBOROUGH UNITED	4
BRISTOL ROVERS	6	PLYMOUTH ARGYLE	8
BURNLEY	9	PORTSMOUTH	3
BURY	1	PRESTON	6
CARDIFF CITY	7	QUEENS PARK RANGERS	6
CARLISLE UNITED	5	READING	5
CHARLTON ATHLETIC	7	ROCHDALE	2
CHELSEA	2	SCUNTHORPE	2
COLCHESTER UNITED	6	SHEFFIELD UNITED	3
COVENTRY CITY	7	SHEFFIELD WEDNESDAY	8
CRYSTAL PALACE	7	SHREWSBURY TOWN	1
DAGENHAM & REDBRIDGE	2	SOUTHEND UNITED	3
DERBY COUNTY	7	STOCKPORT	2
DONCASTER ROVERS	4	STOKE CITY	7
EVERTON	2	SUNDERLAND	5

EXETER CITY	3	SWANSEA CITY	2
FULHAM	1	SWINDON TOWN	5
GILLINGHAM	2	TORQUAY UNITED	2
HARTLEPOOL UNITED	4	TOTTENHAM HOTSPUR	1
HUDDERSFIELD TOWN	4	TRANMERE ROVERS	3
HULL CITY	6	WALSALL	3
IPSWICH TOWN	9	WATFORD	6
LEEDS UNITED	5	WEST BROMWICH ALBION	3
LEICESTER CITY	7	WEST HAM UNITED	2
LEYTON ORIENT	4	WIGAN ATHLETIC	1
LUTON TOWN	2	WOLVERHAMPTON WANDERERS	5
MANCHESTER CITY	3	WYCOMBE WANDERERS	1
MANCHESTER UNITED	2	YEOVIL TOWN	6

The club historians get requests for information from all sorts of sources both inside and outside the club but it was novel for them to get an enquiry from the club President Terry Paine, on behalf of Kelvin.

They had been sitting together watching a match when Kelvin had asked Terry where he thought he might stand in the list of appearances for the club. Terry asked the historians and David Bull and Gary Chalk were able to tell Kelvin that he was just behind a group of players who he could probably overtake in the course of the next season but he would have to go some to pass Tommy Allen, the all-time holder with 327 appearances in the 1920s. Kelvin then played enough games the following season to overtake the post-war goalkeepers in rapid succession.

In an FA Cup match at home against Chelsea on New Year's Day 2014 Kelvin passed the post-war goalkeeping record of 289 appearances held by Eric Martin. By this time, he had set his sights firmly on reaching 300 appearances although he was resigned to the likelihood of not beating the all-time record of Tommy Allen.

He reached 300 appearances on the last game of the 2014-15 season Premier League at Manchester City. Here are the milestones on his way to 300 appearances.

50	**BARNSLEY**	Home	**22 September 2007**
100	**READING**	Away	**22 November 2008**
150	**NORWICH CITY**	Home	**21 November 2009**
200	**PETERBOROUGH UNITED**	Home	**20 November 2010**
250	**PORTSMOUTH**	Away	**18 December 2011**
300	**MANCHESTER CITY**	Away	**24 May 2015**

Life Outside Football

Clearly, football is central to Kelvin's life but his family is just as important, perhaps even more so. The happiness of his wife Kelly and their three children is paramount to him.

In order to understand the kind of man he is it seems right to give the first words to Kelly.

They met at Brooklands Middle school in Leighton Buzzard. Kelvin was in Kelly's friendship group which was not difficult given that he was friendly with most people.

Kelvin left school and went to do his apprenticeship in Luton but he and Kelly kept in touch. Kelly was attending college in Luton which was just down the road from Kelvin so they would meet occasionally but as Kelly puts it, *"We were still just friends from school really".*

Kelvin would return to his family home some weekends and Kelly would go and see him, together with Kelvin's best friend. Their relationship blossomed and in June 2001 they were married at All Saints church, a *"lovely church"* in Leighton Buzzard. For them it is the family church where Kelly's parents got married. Kelly, her sister and brother were all christened there, as were Kelvin's and Kelly's three children, Emelia (13), Sonnie (11), and three-year-old Buddy. Amusingly, Kelvin says that the arrival of Buddy has meant that he has had to get out of the habit of affectionately calling people 'Bud' or 'Buddy'.

When he got married Kelvin was playing for Wimbledon and any thoughts about the significance of the name *All Saints* were non-existent.

....

Talking about Kelvin, the man outside football, the first word that comes to Kelly's mind is *"funny",* reflecting the fun and laughter that Kelvin can generate at home.

She quickly adds *"thoughtful"* as one of his main attributes. As he himself has revealed he is definitely a family man before everything else and family time is truly important to him.

According to Kelly Kelvin likes springing surprises and making people laugh. She reveals the most shocking thing he used to do but she is quick to stress that he no longer does it. When they were younger and they were at the home of Kelly's Mum Val and Dad Pat, Kelvin was known to go upstairs and then reappear wearing Val's clothes. On one occasion when they were on holiday he emerged wearing Val's swimming costume. But now any similar sort of behaviour cuts little ice with family and friends because they know that it is standard practice for Kelvin to try to shock. In his defence Kelly adds, *"It's not a bad habit, it is actually quite funny".*

Kelly confirms that everything Kelvin does is carefully thought out and although he was not so calm when he was younger, *"now he's quite calm".*

He definitely judges people by the impression they make on him and not by what somebody else has told him. He is known for invariably seeing the good in people and even if someone is really annoying him he always tries to see the positive in that person.

However, he can become irritated, as demonstrated by a couple of incidents related elsewhere in this book. Anyone who does succeed in making him angry must soon realise that they have overstepped the mark because he is normally so calm and *"chilled out".* If he shows that he does not like someone or they have upset him, Kelly says *"they must have really upset him".* Having said all that, he is tolerant and does not like to hold grudges, preferring to clear the air.

....

Kelly's recollections of the JPT final have been described earlier and for her and all the family it was a particularly special occasion and atmosphere. In general, she enjoys watching him play and is always completely confident, stating that she has more confidence in him than anyone else.

Despite her confidence, she confesses that she is *"ridiculously nervous"* and perhaps has become more so over the years that she has known him and watched him play. If he has not played for a while she feels anxious and sickly on his return. But this is nothing to do with his ability, or doubting his ability and what he might do. Her worry is more about what might happen if things do not go to plan in the game and in particular she worries about what reaction he might get from the fans. She doesn't like hearing criticism of her husband and that is what really makes her nervous.

While Kelvin has some negative moments with fans he is *Super Kelvin Davis* for so many of them and Kelly feels good that the fans really support him. She says, *"I've had odd Southampton fans that have said things. But mostly I always sense that they enjoy it when he's playing and they're confident like I am".*

Kelly hears people say *"lovely things"* about her husband but she admits that perhaps some of the compliments are lost on her because she is so close to him anyway. She enjoys it when she hears the praise even though it can be surprising, a little embarrassing and humbling because at home they just get on with their family life. At home Kelly thinks of him as *"just Kelvin".* She and the family are living their life and Kelvin is doing his job and that's all there is to it. As Kelly sees it, *"Kelvin is part of the team and most supporters probably like all or most of the players in the team".*

....

Kelvin often talks about team spirit and community spirit, both of which he values highly. At Southampton he has been able to experience and has been responsible for the close community that there is, especially for the wives, girlfriends and partners of the players.

Kelly finds it difficult to explain why that was, although one factor was that they all had young children. As she says, *"We just all got on, the wives and the players. Most weekends after a game it was almost automatic for people to do stuff together or you'd go out for dinner together".* There is no doubt that it was a bonus that the players and their loved ones all got on so well. Kelly likes to think that being such good friends off the pitch helped on the pitch when the players found themselves *"playing for a mate who is also a team mate".*

....

Among the highlights in Kelvin's career Kelly remembers in particular when he signed his professional contract, although she admits that she probably failed to understand just how significant it was at the time. She recalls when Kelvin first went from Luton to Wimbledon. It was a move to a bigger club because Wimbledon were bigger at the time. *"We were really young and moving away from home and all those kinds of things. It sticks with me and it was character-building".*

As she looks back there have been so many moments to cherish even though she had to make do with listening to the Plymouth promotion game on the radio, at home with her young family. Once again it was the closeness of the group that made the occasion feel even more special because *"The girls were together listening to every goal that went in and we felt part of it".*

....

Everyone who is asked their opinion of Kelvin Davis replies in glowing terms. But this man cannot be an actual saint as well as a Saint, can he?

His wife Kelly helps to answer by thinking about any down side in his character: *"To say he's a control freak – that's probably a little bit harsh – but he does like to do things his way with regards to organisation. It's probably part of why he's good at what he does. If we're booking a holiday, or if we're looking up flights I'll start the job and then just let him carry on with it. It's not right until he finds a better option. I'm quite happy. If we're in the office doing all the paperwork I just let him do it. He likes to know where everything is. I would say it is a bit of a negative sometimes but not that bad. It's one I can deal with".*

....

Anyone worth their salt (pun intended) has to become a boat owner in Southampton and Kelvin was no exception.

Being down by the water, just like other people, Kelvin fancied buying a little boat and he and his friend Chris Wright did just that. It is interesting that it was in the more modest League One days and not during the more glamourous Championship or Premier League days. The little boat (called 'Looking Forward') was meant to be a taster with the intention, or the dream, of getting a bigger and better one in the years ahead. Kelvin did enjoy it but he had insufficient time to get out and make the most of it, joking that to get the most out of a boat, *"You need to have a job where you work from home or on a boat".*

Anyway, off they went towards Cowes on their maiden voyage when all of a sudden the engine cut out and they found themselves bobbing around halfway between Southampton and the Isle of Wight. Their many attempts to restart it were a failure and all they could do was to drop anchor in the middle of the Solent, sitting right in the path of the Red Funnel ferries which were coming and going past them. As the ferries passed they seemed to be looking at the stranded sailors as much to say, *"What are you doing?"* Eventually the intrepid sailors had to call out Sea Start who provide marine breakdown assistance and they towed the hapless voyagers back to Southampton. So it was that Kelvin's future career as a round-the-world sailor faltered, *"We had another couple of trips on it and then that was it".*

....

A highly significant interest which takes Kelvin away from football is the Southampton-based organisation Liver and Pancreatic Research and Development Charity, referred to as LAP for short. It is important to Kelvin that people know about the background to the charity which was established by patients in 2012. It has one overriding aim: to improve patient care and work together to beat liver and pancreatic cancer.

Liver and pancreatic cancer affects more than 15,000 patients in the UK every year. Unlike many other forms of cancer, detection and cure rates for liver and pancreatic cancer have not improved in the last 40 years. The charity funds research that detects the early signs of these forms of cancer and enhances mini-invasive treatment and after care methods.

The Southampton Hepatobiliary Pancreatic Team performs more than 250 major procedures every year for liver and pancreatic malignancies with the majority being via keyhole surgery. The Team recognised the need to create a charitable fund to develop surgical techniques further and to ensure they become more widely available with a positive impact on both patients and their families.

LAP is supported by an enthusiastic group of medical practitioners, patients, family members and friends who are dedicated to help and support people affected by these serious conditions.

It was as a result of Kelly being unwell that initially moved Kelvin to get involved with the charity. Kelly had appendicitis but unfortunately she developed complications and became seriously ill. Her surgeon was Mr Mohammed Abu Hilal who had to perform an operation that would normally take 20 minutes but which lasted over three hours, all of this happening on New Year's Eve.

Mo' Hilal was a founder member of the LAP charity and knowing that Kelvin was very grateful for Kelly's treatment and recovery, he seized the opportunity to seek a little help. Mo simply asked Kelvin if he could donate a signed Southampton shirt that might be auctioned in aid of the charity. Those who know Kelvin will not be surprised that he did not let it rest at that. As he got to understand more about what the charity was seeking to do, his interest became much wider, and he is now fully committed to backing the work of the charity. As he has become more and more involved he has built up a rewarding relationship with the people who run the charity. Kelly adds that when Kelvin speaks about the charity in public people really do listen both because *"he is interesting"* and because *"he is genuine and sincere".*

Kelvin became the patron of the charity in February 2015. Sadly, in January 2016 a founding member and chairman of the charity, John Burke, passed away. Kelvin was invited to take over as chairman and he readily agreed.

Most of all Kelvin has been able to nurture the partnership that was already in place between LAP and the Saints Foundation. In the 2014-15 season the Saints Foundation raised £20,000 for the charity through a series of activities, including a sky dive, fundraising at the Player Awards Dinner and sales of a number of player-worn signed shirts.

Liver and
Pancreatic R&D
CANCER CHARITY

Anyone interested in finding out more about how to support Kelvin's favoured charity should go to the website: http://www.lapcancercharity.com/

What Kelvin Says

Many tributes have been made to Kelvin and these will undoubtedly continue and culminate in a collective tribute at his testimonial match. In addition to his obvious indebtedness to his goalkeeping coaches, Kelvin wants to celebrate a number of fine working relationships that he has enjoyed with people who he has worked with and who have supported in different ways.

....

It would be remiss, to say the least if this section did not start with Kelvin's reflection on the man who quite literally saved Southampton Football Club: the late **Markus Liebherr.**

Kelvin does not hesitate to express his heartfelt thanks to Markus who he says helped him to *"fulfil his dream in so many ways".* Markus showed his commitment and belief in the club when he bought it and the Saints' supporters still acknowledge how important Markus was to the club. Kelvin says how touching it is to hear fans express their admiration and gratitude with chants of *"one Markus Liebherr"* and *"walking in a Liebherr wonderland"* at both home and away games.

Kelvin recalls the first time that he met Markus at St Mary's. He was asked by Nicola Cortese to take a shirt signed by the squad to the board room and to present it to the new owner. Markus was there with some members of his family and Kelvin was slightly nervous about what he might say.

As he handed over the shirt, which was large enough to fit Markus, Kelvin spotted a tray of biscuits on the board room table. Without thinking he heard himself saying, *"You won't be needing any more biscuits".* Markus was a man of few words but he smiled and said quietly, *"No, you are probably right".* Kelvin had got away with it once again.

Kelvin also praises **Katharina Liebherr** who had to take the reins so suddenly when Markus passed away. *"She still has her father's spirit and always has the best interests of the club in her heart".*

One person who has been a constant during Kelvin's time at Southampton is **Ros Wheeler**, the club secretary. Some of the key directors when Kelvin first signed were destined to leave over time but Ros has remained and over the years Kelvin has built up a strong working relationship with her, based on mutual respect.

At the start of his time as a Saint Kelvin admits to not really knowing what her role was. She was based at the training ground and the only time he had any contact with her was *"about tickets and that kind of thing"*. Gradually Kelvin realised that Ros was an important point of contact, working as she did alongside Rupert Lowe. When he left the club and it went into administration Kelvin holds the view that Ros was *"more or less running the club"*. The decisions she made at that time show that her heart and soul is in Southampton Football Club and that she always wants what will be the best for the club.

Fortunately, Ros had seen his passion for the club having been involved in meetings where he had spoken about the importance of trying to stay up and not being relegated. He had been relegated before and he was always pointing out that *"it is something that stays with you. You felt like you'd got to the end of battle and lost. It stains you and it's hard to wash off"*.

Ros was alongside Kelvin, and other players, all the way through the period of administration and she was the key point of contact for Kelvin in the difficult situation he found himself in. The working relationship had grown and came to fruition when the situation came up with West Ham in the summer of administration. Ros knew exactly the situation for Kelvin, in terms of him being out of contract. They spoke almost every other day as to when the club might be taken over, while Kelvin was training with West Ham who had made an offer for him.

When the takeover had eventually been agreed Ros phoned him as he finished training at West Ham and told him that the new owners wanted him to stay and that a contract was ready for him to sign.

Kelvin says that it felt as if he had never really left as he hurried down to Hampshire to sign the contract. Smiling he says, *"I don't know who was happier at the time, me or*

Kelly or Ros". That was the start of an even stronger relationship and from that point Kelvin looked upon Ros as his *"go to"* person.

The tribute to Ros is best in Kelvin's own words, *"She's always there and what I like most about Ros is that she doesn't always give you the answer you want. She gives you the honest answer. You need that and every football club needs a Ros because she genuinely cares about every employee at the club".*

With his look of boyish mischief Kelvin suggests that her husband would be the first to say that he's down the pecking order, *"First it's the football club and then it's him. I don't think he'd have it any other way and certainly she's a massive influence on the football club and why it's where it is now".*

....

Amongst many people who can take the plaudits for the club being where it is now is the one-time Executive Chairman, **Nicola Cortese**. As club captain Kelvin found he had a good working relationship with Nicola.

At the time he came to Southampton Football Club it needed strong leadership and vision. As club captain Kelvin was fortunate enough to work more closely with Nicola than some others. Although his leadership style may not have been to everyone's taste the fact remains that he did a huge amount to give the club a strong direction and a heightened profile in the football world.

Looking back now there was a *"great moment",* as Kelvin calls it, that confirmed that Nicola and Kelvin were both very serious about the club going forward and getting it back to where they felt it should be and could be.

This *"great moment"* came during a discussion involving Nicola Cortese, Dean Hammond and Kelvin. The chairman was *"quite disgruntled about the result and the performance"* away at Wycombe Wanderers the evening before – the result was 0-0. In the meeting Nicola asked questions as to *"why we didn't go to Wycombe and win".* Kelvin became uncomfortable feeling that no professional *"goes out to not perform or to not play well"* and that *"you step out on the pitch and you try and win a game of football"*.

At some stage in the conversation Kelvin was moved to say, *"Nicola, I didn't give up the opportunity to play in the Premier League with West Ham to sit in League One for the rest of my career".* He leaned over and said, *"Kelvin, I didn't give up my nice life in Switzerland to run a League One club".* From that point onwards there was a mutual respect with many conversations on different subjects.

Kelvin knew that it was very unusual for players to discuss football or team issues directly with the chairman. It was a positive for Kelvin to have direct links *"as long as you did it responsibly".* Even seemingly small issues might be discussed because they were big issues for the players. Kelvin raised the fact that the team used to travel around the country on an uncomfortable bus, *"Mr Chairman, we're not happy with our bus".* The reply was *"Okay, we'll get you a better bus"* … and it was done.

....

Kelvin likes to stress that although he has talked about *"disappointment"* and *"confusion",* it was a very small part of **Nigel Adkins's** time at the club. Coming to Southampton could have been seen as a step up for Nigel but Kelvin recognises that he came into a club which *"had the players and had the set-up".* Kelvin sums up Nigel's management style, *"He organised the team very well. Sometimes the best management style is to sit back and lay the seeds, lay a format and let the players go and finish the job".*

In the League One and the Championship campaigns there were a lot of games to play. It can be very difficult to manage and prepare for the following game in a short time but Nigel's strategy between games was very, very good. There is no doubt that all the players and staff felt the pressure in League One because the club was expected to *"walk the league".* Kelvin had an overwhelming feeling about the promotion from League One. It was the *"relief"* of promotion rather than the elation of promotion. When promotion from the Championship came, *"it was nice to come off the pitch and celebrate with the team and shake the manager's hand in a manner that was a job well done. And it was".*

At the end of season awards evening Kelvin recalls something that Nigel said that won him much respect. During the evening Nigel was interviewed and one of the questions was *"Have you thought about any players for next season?"* As a member of the team that got the club promoted Kelvin found it an impolite question by talking about what players are going to be replaced while everyone is at a celebratory evening. Kelvin admired Nigel for his answer, *"Let's worry about that another day. Tonight's about celebrating what these players have done".* That is certainly a side of Nigel that Kelvin has a lot of respect for.

Kelvin sums up Nigel's positive qualities, *"He was never a tea-cup thrower and he was always very calm. I think that he was always very positive. Even when you knew he wasn't in a positive frame of mind he always tried to show a positive attitude".*

Kelvin is unable to resist sharing another moment that has stuck in his mind from the awards evening. There were to be fireworks at one stage during the event and Danny Butterfield had a fantastic whistle that he managed to echo through the stand. This got some people going, especially those who had enjoyed a couple of glasses of champagne, and they thought the fireworks had started.

....

First impressions count a lot for Kelvin and he is clear that **Alan Pardew** got a lot of respect from him as a result of their first conversation. He phoned Kelvin on the day he got the job and was the first manager ever to do that. His first thought on coming in was to touch base with the captain. He might have also spoken to other experienced pros at the club at the time but Kelvin points out that *"there weren't too many left at that point".*

They had a half-hour chat on the way Kelvin saw things and what his thoughts were. Kelvin came off the phone feeling positive. He felt that Pardew had shown that he was going to treat him with that level of respect from the outset. This is not to say that later on they would not have disagreements but the bottom line was that the opening dialogue was very positive and *"For me it was a great statement for the club to bring in a manager of that calibre".*

Part of his management style was to treat the experienced pros with a lot of respect and they all felt that *"we were on the right path".* Even at that early stage Pardew had a clear idea of the type of player who he wanted to bring to the club. The signings he made when he was at the club are evidence of his good judgement with Lambert being the standout candidate.

Beating Bristol Rovers 4-0 was a result that the players felt was really going to kick-start the campaign but Kelvin was as surprised as everyone when he came in on the Monday morning. After being told on the Saturday that he would not be needed to play on the Tuesday night in the JPT he learned that he would play after all.

At the training ground on the Monday morning Kelvin was told that Nicola was waiting to see him to talk about who was going to take over the role for the foreseeable future and until a new manager was appointed, following Pardew's sacking.

Kelvin stresses that the positives in Alan Pardew outweighed the negatives but there were a couple. On one occasion following a win at home he beckoned me with *"the little curly finger and the nod of his head".* Pardew said, *"You look like you're showing off a bit in goal",* implying that when Kelvin was taking goal kicks the manager felt that he *"wasn't fully focused on the game".*

Kelvin replied, *"Alan, I really need you to explain that to me better. I really don't understand what you're asking me to do".* Kelvin has tried for a long time to understand what he meant with his next comment, *"Well, when you're playing, just have a little bit less X factor".*

The only possible explanation is that the fans were very supportive of Kelvin and Pardew did not understand why and, *"I think he thought I was playing up to them a bit".*

Kelvin cannot talk about Alan Pardew and ignore the fact that he took the team captain's armband from Kelvin, who does admit that he saw it coming. *"Some managers have a problem with the goalkeeper wearing the arm band, some managers don't like it at all. When Nigel came in he preferred Dean Hammond having the arm band because of him being in a central location and felt that he could manage the game better".*

The decision was communicated to Kelvin when the manager called him to the office and handed him his programme notes for the coming Saturday. It explained that although Kelvin will always be the club captain the team captain arm band was being given to Dean Hammond.

Understandably, Kelvin was upset about the decision but he respects the fact that *"he pulled me to the side, he told me like a man, his reasons were valid".*

The line that Kelvin came out with stands as testimony to the man, *"I don't care whether I've got the armband or not. You don't need an armband to be a captain".*

....

Kelvin claims not to remember too much about **George Burley** saying, *"It was bloody ages ago".* It might be less the passage of time and more about the fact that Kelvin did not then hold the captaincy responsibilities and therefore did not enjoy that closer relationship with the manager. He does say that any player has a lot of respect for the manager who has signed him, *"You know that they've put their head on the block for you, if you like, and put their hand up for you. You've joined a club with their full support".*

There was only one occasion when Kelvin found his respect for Burley being challenged. There had been an incident in a game against Birmingham City in November 2006. Although the Saints won 4-3, Radhi Jaidi, then of Birmingham, headed a late goal that went in due to confusion between Kelvin and defender Chris Baird. Kelvin might have made the save but Baird just touched the ball which sent it over Kelvin into the net.

Kelvin looked at his team mate and gave a shrug of his shoulders because there was nothing that they could have done. However, Baird reacted to the shrug and started to *"have a go"* at Kelvin which incensed him. He says he had it out with Baird but is keen to stress that it was a one-off incident which has not affected their relationship in the long term. Kelvin felt that he was totally in the right and says that he *"lost a bit of respect for the manager who appeared to side with his defender"*.

Characteristically Kelvin finds positives in George Burley, who had a certain way that he wanted to play and was both adamant and clear as to what should happen. Kelvin admired the way Burley worked with the team when they did set plays on a Friday. Often he would put the ball in the box and cross the ball into wide spaces because he wanted to demonstrate with his delivery precisely where he wanted the ball and what sort of ball he wanted.

Kelvin recalls how Burley managed situations rather than individual players or people, leaving that side to his staff. Kelvin does not doubt the potential for success that he brought and the players who came in all had one thing in mind which was to get promoted. Unfortunately they were not.

....

The first meeting Kelvin had with **Mauricio Pochettino** was, in his words, *"a little bit similar to the Pardew situation"*. He tells how he, Rickie Lambert, Adam Lallana, and José Fonte were called to the club and asked to wait in one of the executive boxes at the stadium. Kelvin was late for the meeting because there was a heavy snowfall and the management team were also running late because of the difficulties getting to the ground. They waited for about 20 minutes and then it was announced that the chairman Nicola Cortese would be joining them to introduce the new manager. As with any such first meeting the players were keen to make a good first impression.

When the new team came in Kelvin says that *"you knew instantly that they were extremely professional and very together as a group. I think we all left that meeting with a positive mind"*. Kelvin felt that the first statement of intent was very clear. A seven-

or ten-day mid-season break had been planned *"in some hot climate somewhere"*. But Mauricio Pochettino said *"No. We're going to go to Barcelona"*. At the time Barcelona was place to go, almost the heart of football. The manager had lived there and knew it very well, so he was comfortable with taking the squad there.

The squad worked solidly for four or five days running through how the manager wanted them to play, with different ways of attacking and playing out from the back. Kelvin and the other players *"felt straightaway that we were in good hands, in the company of people that know their job. A lot of things changed from that day. Every training session was videoed"*.

Mauricio had a purpose-built office which replaced the office in the little farmhouse that previous managers had occupied. It was not a case of it not being good enough in terms of their status but they simply felt that the previous building was not suited to the way they wanted to operate.

In the new shared office Mauricio had a seat by the window and Kelvin recalls that when *"you walked by the window you got the nod that said 'Come in. Come in' and when you go in the office he'd be there watching and reviewing the training sessions that we'd done that day. They were always looking for ways to improve – not just to improve as individuals, not just to improve as a team but also themselves"*.

Kelvin feels that this was *"the new level, when we felt as players that this was the step up, this was the progression. Any doubts that Nicola had not made the right decision and any doubts that we weren't heading in the right direction were dispelled"*.

Kelvin enjoyed a good relationship and acknowledges that Mauricio was very personal and a different type of man manager. He wanted to get to know you as a person. Although his English was not perfect at the time Kelvin says that he would often describe someone as a *"good person"* which meant that above all else he was someone that Mauricio wanted to know. For him it was not about football ability alone, it was also about the man. The coaching staff he had around him were all very similar characters and the players really felt that they had the nucleus of a powerful group.

When Mauricio and his team left after a highly successful season there was disappointment all round and this was made worse by departures of key players. Kelvin was particularly disappointed to get a call from Rickie Lambert to say that he was going to join Liverpool. While he didn't begrudge Rickie the chance to join his home town club he felt *"gutted"* for himself in that his close friend was leaving.

However, Kelvin recalls how his spirits were lifted when he got a call from Executive Director **Les Reed** to let him know that the club had appointed **Ronald Koeman** as manager. Kelvin felt that this showed the ambition and status of the club and he says that *"Ronald and his team have shown him nothing but respect during their time at the club"*. That sense of respect is mutual and Kelvin especially wants to place on record his gratitude to Ronald and his management team for the enthusiastic support they are giving to his testimonial match.

Les Reed is one of two other people for whom Kelvin continues to have great respect, the other being Chairman **Ralph Krueger.** Les has *"done everything in football and has been the knowledge and vision behind the club's recent success"* whilst Kelvin likes *"the way Ralph is always upbeat and positive and is able to instil belief in the potential of the club and everyone connected with it".*

Kelvin is particularly grateful to Ralph and Les for their close support and for working with him closely as he approaches the next stage in his career. Both men recognise that Kelvin fully shares their ambitions for the club.

A future role for Kelvin is not confirmed but the three of them have a working relationship which Kelvin knows could continue to grow and which might offer him a place in the *"fantastic future"* of the club.

What Other People Say

A lot has been written about Kelvin's relationships with coaches and other staff who have helped him to achieve what he wanted to achieve over his ten seasons at Southampton. But Kelvin looked surprised when he learned that tributes would be included in his book and he is not a man who displays false modesty. But one of the contributors, Dave Merrington, insisted that it is *"crucial"* for the book to include the accolades that Kelvin deserves. This is an opportunity to hear and feel what people say about their admiration and respect for Super Kel.

The tributes that follow have been put forward by players, former colleagues, supporters, family and others who know Kelvin well. In the time available to produce this book it has not been possible to contact everybody who has figured in Kelvin's life and career but the tributes collected strike a consistent note about his work ethic, his sense of humour and his caring nature.

Do not be alarmed if some of the tributes read like an obituary. Kelvin is definitely alive and kicking. It's all to do with his glutes.

These tributes appear here not only for today's readers but also as a record for the future, when Kelvin will want to look back with his children, or even his grandchildren, and share with them the real affection and respect that he has engendered in people in and around Southampton.

....

FORMER TEAM MATES AND COLLEAGUES

Dan Harding is not only a former team mate but also a close friend and still a neighbour of Kelvin. He thinks first about Kelvin as captain and starts with the accolade that all the lads *"respected Kelvin from the youth team right up to the big boys in the first team"*. If anyone stepped out of line or something was not done properly

Kelvin would have a quiet word. He might do it so discreetly that other players would be unaware of it. Dan describes a fantastic squad of good professionals and because of the respect and esteem he enjoyed Kelvin could say anything, on the pitch or off the pitch, and the squad listened and took notice.

Any of the players could go to Kelvin for advice about non-footballing matters, such as how to get car insurance or how to go about buying the car they want, Kelvin was always open to being asked for guidance or advice on a number of problems, some of which were relatively minor. Dan knows of captains in the past who have taken advantage of the situation, even financially, by *"putting them in touch with certain people and thank you very much for that"*. Kelvin made it clear that he would never ever give advice that would lead to his own financial gain.

Dan is certain that success of the team was also about the enjoyment they got from spending time with each other. Everyone had the hunger and desire to do well out on the pitch but they also wanted to spend time with each other away from the club. Kelvin was a strong catalyst for the bond the players and their families enjoyed then and which has continued to today.

One of the disappointments for Kelvin was when he had the team captaincy taken from him and he went from being both club and team captain to being just the club captain. However, Dan believes that people still saw him as the captain and he still did the role that he has always done. In a similar situation some players might have thought, *"Hold on, you're pushing me out a little bit but you're still expecting me to do it, to do all the stuff that I did before"* but it is not in Kelvin's nature to think that way and that served simply to enhance his standing in the dressing room.

"He was by far the best Captain I've ever had in terms of what he allowed to happen in the changing room. For example, as a group of footballers there are certain things that are accepted and not accepted and we were a fantastic team and a fantastic unit. We had a cohesiveness that I've never really had anywhere.

I've got the utmost respect for him. There's Kelvin the man as well. I think it rolls in with the captaincy thing, you know, everyone at the club also has the utmost respect for him. I think he's always been the father figure, the elder of the squad, of the team. But don't get me wrong Kelvin would be having the most fun as well. Although he was that figure head he didn't have a problem going out and having a beer with the younger lads or giving them advice. There was none of that "I'm club captain" and the stigma that comes around it".

Dan recalls a lot of changing room banter which you might not expect from a senior professional but Kelvin was never shy of promoting the innocent fun that used to go on and Dan feels that such lighter moments actually increased the unity of the team. If Kelvin was not directly involved, he was nearly always instrumental in something that was going on. He might not have been the sole perpetrator but he would normally have been the brains behind the idea.

It is possible that some fans only see one side of Kelvin – the serious Kelvin who is so highly focused on winning. Fans are unlikely to see his lighter side that his team mates experience at the training ground or even away from it. The team would regularly hold social occasions, such as a barbecue, and Dan describes how, *"On one such occasion we were all in his garden and Kelvin went off for about 20 minutes. We all wondered where he had gone and eventually he arrived having driven his car round the back of the garden just to give everyone a laugh".*

Although fans might not see this lighter side they did witness it at the beginning of the new season when he was filmed driving his car repeatedly round and round the roundabout at the entrance to the training complex. Perhaps it was Kelvin posing an unspoken question *"Am I staying or am I going?"*

Kelvin tries to deny that he is a practical joker but he did like the fines system. He used to take a players' meeting on a Friday before training when he would dish out fines. For example, players had to pay for transgressions like forgetting their kit, or wearing someone else's kit or boots, or for wearing flip flops in the shower.

There were also two areas in the shower, an area where players were allowed to do a wee and another section where they were forbidden to do a wee. Kelvin would issue fines for anyone breaking the rule although he will not reveal how he knew who had committed the wicked deed.

Another way of imposing fines was by making the players' own meeting overrun, leading to people being late for the scheduled first team meeting for which there was another fine. Kelvin says with a smile that the money used to go to *"charity"*. In truth, Kelvin used to save it for the Christmas do.

One particularly memorable Christmas party was held in a dirty and dingy place in Brighton. One of the lads said to Rickie Lambert, *"How high can you jump, Rick?"*

He said, *"Quite high".*

"Show us then".

So he did. Rickie jumped up and hit his head on the low ceiling. He only banged his head but Kelvin and Dan agree that this was apparently *"a normal night out for Rickie".*

....

The bang on the head was not the first incident or accident involving Rickie. The club were on a pre-season trip to Switzerland and after their final match on the Saturday they were told by the manager that they would train the next day and then they could *"let their hair down a bit"* in the evening. Kelvin and his room-mate Rickie decided that they would "escape" the hotel and go into the town for the Light Festival. In order to get out without being noticed they knew they could climb over the balcony of the room of Jos Hooiveld and Steven ("Wonder") Davis.

Jos and Steven decided to join Kelvin and Rickie for what turned out to be a highly entertaining evening which eventually led to a few drinks in a bar in the town. At one point Rickie went to sit down at their table but half-missed the chair. Reaching out to stop himself falling on the floor Rickie's hand landed on a glass which smashed and, not surprisingly, gave him a nasty gash.

The four decided that stitches might be needed and they should get back to the team hotel, bearing in mind that on their return Rickie would not be able to make his way over the balcony. When they got to the hotel Kelvin tried calling the physio but there was no reply, which was hardly surprising at 3.00 a.m. Kelvin then called the club doctor who answered quickly, having guessed that something was amiss.

Eventually Rickie was helped to the doctor's room and he confirmed that he would need to stitch the wound. The low lighting in the hotel room made this difficult so they would have to rely on a torch from a mobile phone, the only available one being on Rickie's. The problem was that the torch only functioned in the SOS mode so the doctor had to struggle to stitch and dress the wound as the light flashed S O S.

As Kelvin says, *"What goes on tour, stays on tour"* … until now.

....

On these painful notes it seems only right to give **Rickie Lambert** the chance to pay his tribute to his close friend in his own words.

"I remember first meeting him when I was playing for Bristol Rovers. That was a massive game for us, in the FA Cup. I got the only goal from a free kick and I didn't actually make good contact but I think it hit Wright and deflected in. I know how much that hurt him.

When I arrived at Southampton I've got to say that I really looked up to Kelvin. He had such a presence in the club. As for my first impressions I was taken aback but he really helped me to fit into the club. He is so dedicated, an ace professional but that doesn't stop him having a laugh. He can go from serious to funny very quickly. He's got a ruthless sense of humour but he wouldn't want to hurt anybody.

I found this out when he took me to the dressing room on my first day. He showed me my position and I put my stuff there. Then as the players arrived they shook hands and that but they were all sniggering. I found out why when one of the other strikers came in – it was Saganowski – and he looked puzzled because I was in his position. He took it okay but Kelvin had well and truly set me up.

But don't get me wrong, he knows when to be a serious professional. There are lots of words you could use about him – dedicated, hard-working, very fit and focused. For me, a man of steel. He is honestly the best goalkeeper I've ever played with and I will never forget that freak of a night – Leeds away. But it was not only that night – he won us so many points.

He didn't have any weaknesses on the pitch although I moaned at him if he didn't kick the ball over my right shoulder. He will go on about his goal assists, like the one at Brighton. And what about his pass that helped me get my volley at MK Dons?

He's so loved and respected in the game and among his friends. At Rovers I was used to going out with the lads but it was so different at Southampton. With us all living pretty close to each other he used to get all the lads together at his place for barbecues and the like so that we could let our hair down together. A true captain and terrific family man who loves Kelly and his kids. When I left Southampton I missed him a lot. A true friend.

So what about the future? I think he can do whatever he wants. He could be a coach or even an assistant manager, and probably go on to be a manager at some time. The club has to keep him. I love the man".

....

Defender **Jos Hooiveld** is another former team mate who has remained a good friend of Kelvin. From his days spent with Kelvin at Southampton, Jos remembers there being two sides to Kelvin's personality.

"The funny side with the jokes and the banter but also the caring side. I will give an example of both things.

I will always remember the fines on Friday, it was always a great little meeting before the training and often Steve de Ridder had to pay the most. Kelv was the perfect host for that. But the best example of Kelv and his banter was the barbecue at his place. Everyone got invited and the wives and girlfriends were there. It was a warm day and Kelv was operating as the chef. After a few minutes he went missing and came back in an amazing outfit. Let's describe it like this: he wasn't wearing much, but still he managed to come out with a tail like a dog. You had to see the faces of everyone. Brilliant!

The caring side: the first day of training when I came to Saints we played 11-a-side. There was a discussion between me and what I thought was a mouthy young kid. I told him to pipe down and to go on … in not the friendliest words. Kelv pulled me later and said, just let him get off the hook, he is our best player. The kid was Adam Lallana ha ha! Another example was when I had the own goals fever. A few times Kelv took me and we went for a coffee, just to sit and talk about all sorts of things. Just to get my head right. We had a good understanding me and Kelv. Will defo see him again after football".

....

A former room-mate of Kelvin is **Paul Wotton** who recalls why he has remained such a close family friend.

"When I first joined Southampton Kelv was one of the first players I met. He'd been there ages. Our families and children got on really well and he's turned into one of my best mates in football. We just clicked straightaway with our similar sense of humour. We became room-mates and he was brilliant.

Our children went to school with Emelia and Sonnie and they are really close as well. They are up there for half term and they'll all be there for his testimonial night. I'll definitely be there – it'll be a good night although I need to lose about a stone in weight.

On a more serious note he really is one of the best professionals I've ever played with in terms of work rate and how professionally he goes about things. He's a fantastic leader as well and it was a pleasure to play with him. He fully deserves everything he gets because he's a top man.

He could be serious when the situation called for it but he was never short of a joke or a prank, again when the time was right. Kelvin was always at the centre of the banter but when it came to work time, Kelvin's work time, he was probably one of the most dedicated goalkeepers I've played with. His work rate and his work ethic never flagged. I remember we went out on a Thursday afternoon and I flogged myself to death doing crossing and I said, "Oi, it's Thursday afternoon". "But it's something we've got to do". The best goalie I've played with, by a mile.

In the first season I had at Southampton under the Dutch manager he was outstanding. People might forget that, even though we got relegated, Kelvin kept us in games single-handedly at times. He was fantastic.

He enjoyed a joke in the dressing room but he never wound me up because we were partners in crime most of the time. We had good fun at the expense of Papa Waigo and Radhi Jaidi but, although it was never hurtful, I'm not really sure if we can describe them in a book that will be read by fans of different ages and backgrounds.

His work ethic and sense of dedication came a lot from his family background plus the fact that he's from that era when we were apprentices. Things were different to how they are nowadays. He's the last of that apprentice era really. We came up through similar clubs – him at Luton and me at Plymouth.

As for his future Kelvin could do anything. If he chose to he could carry on playing at whatever level but not necessarily in the Premier League. He's a fantastic leader and he doesn't shout and bawl but when he says something people respect him and listen. He's respected in the game, he is knowledgeable of football and he's got his head switched on in a business sense. He's not a stereotypical footballer – he's more than that.

If he stays in football he could end up in a role involving contracts and that sort of thing. He always gave good advice when it came to things like that. I think there will definitely be a role for him at Southampton – there has to be.

I don't think you'll get many people saying a bad word about him. I've got lots of things to thank him for both on and off the pitch. He's a real true friend and you don't get many of them in football to be honest with you. No matter what people say – you don't.

He's humble. I know he calls himself Super KD but that's nonsense. He is humble. I couldn't be prouder of him for what he's done. He's a great guy and I am proud to be his friend".

Danny Butterfield is not only Kelvin's friend but the Davis and Butterfield families have stayed close. Here he shares his opinions of Kelvin as well as some amusing stories (including one that is stomach churning) from the time they played together both on and off the pitch.

"I was thinking about playing on the pitch with Kelv and I often had the job, on set pieces, of marking their main centre forward who would be trying to disrupt Kelvin. We had a plan in every game that I would go to trample on the centre forward's toes and Kelv would come across with his elbow. It wasn't meant in a nasty way but just designed to make sure that he didn't get anywhere near Kelv. Building up to each game we'd be deciding who that centre forward was most likely to be and I believe Charlie Austin was one of them. We'd have a chuckle in the dressing room as to which one of them was getting it this week. This is all about Kelv's competitive edge as well as jovial banter during the game.

As a 'keeper you always knew with Kelvin that every single day's training just carried over into a match. He placed a lot of trust in his back four and we knew that if we ever did get beaten we had Kelvin behind us who nine-and-a-half times out of ten would make the save anyway. He was a rock behind the back four and he demanded high standards in front of him. At the same time if we had a slight lapse he always had our backs, he was our 'security man' I suppose.

As a person Kelv loves to be a joker but he's got the knack of being very professional and serious at the right time. He loves to be the main joker and the centre of attention at a party. That's not in an annoying way but if something needed to happen, if the party needed taking up a level to become funny or more exciting the finger normally pointed to me or Kelv or Wotton.

I had only known Kelvin a short time when we went with other families to a barbecue in his garden [the same BBQ that Jos Hooiveld has already mentioned above]. *Kelvin had been ridiculously generous with the food as he always is.*

At one point, Kelvin eventually reappeared from the house completely naked except for his BBQ apron and a pair of shoes. He stood at the barbecue cooking the meat and everything. Bear in mind that my wife had only met him a couple of months before and she couldn't take her eyes off his backside.

Another funny [but less savoury] story happened at the training ground. There was always someone who went in and blocked the toilet in one of the cubicles. We couldn't work out who it was but one of the players had to sit in his car on the drive down from London and then he'd unload when he got to the training ground.

One day Kelv said "It's that massive, it'll never go down the toilet". He decided to get it out and take it to the scales in the physio room and actually weigh it! Bear in mind we were in portacabins at the time and the windows wouldn't open very wide. The whole training ground stank. Kelvin and all the lads were crying with laughter as he tried to weigh it. People were retching while the physios were desperate to get it out of their room.

He never messed about in training but, for example. if we'd had a bad result or something Kelv would remain upbeat to keep everyone's spirits up. As a captain he was a true professional with a mix of humour that allowed the lads to let their hair down at the right time.

His generosity is ridiculous as is his love for Southampton and his team mates. He sees the good in everyone and their positive attributes. He very rarely dwells on the negatives of someone or their performance. He's always thinking about how we can get back to doing the right things to get results.

In the future Kelv could be whatever he wants to be, whatever he sets his heart on – as a manager, as a chief exec, in an ambassador role at Southampton or as a businessman looking at the financial side of football. He's got a wide range of abilities and his personality is that infectious that you buy into whatever his beliefs are. Kelv is capable of anything in any area of football because he is very loyal to what he gets his teeth into and he'll wholeheartedly put great effort into the cause. He is serious and focused but he also has the sense of humour to switch to a less serious role such as corporate hospitality or something as minimal as showing fans around the stadium and telling stories of his playing days, even though he's got a lot more to offer than that.

Kelv's the sort of person that I want to be with, that I want to be around. I can't go too long without being in his company. Our two families are due to go on holiday in the summer. I'll be on a coaching course in the summer so I'll effectively have only two weeks off from football. I could be with just my family but I actually want us to be with Kelv and his family."

....

Lee Holmes has also become a good friend of Kelvin and his family.

"I would say that Kelvin is one of the very few players that I've played with who holds the dressing room so well. He is able to be the joker in and around the dressing room, the life and soul of the team and then when it comes to going onto the training pitch and demanding a performance from himself and the team he is able to switch over to a professionalism that is second to none. He is one of the very few players who can change as quickly as that. It is a real credit to him and where he's taken his career.

We played consistently together for three seasons. Before that I'd never played with a 'keeper who was at their best but Kelv was outstanding, making saves that you just wouldn't expect him to make. I can remember other 'keepers saying "What does Kelvin give you?" The one thing I knew when we were training was that, if I scored a goal it was going to have to be a good goal. If you were shooting against him there were no freebies. He was at the top and that's got him into the position that he is now.

In and around the sport I know other 'keepers who have played a considerable number of games and they relate to Kelvin as the king of the kickers. Not only did he give you his presence as a 'keeper he gave you distribution with his feet. The game was very much about saving shots and protecting your area but there aren't many people who can spray the ball around like Kelvin. He put a massive emphasis on kicking and he made it look easy. For him to be doing that at his age, it was a real privilege to play with him through that period when he was at his peak.

I class him as a very good friend and his family is part of a group of families that have stayed very, very close. In your time in football in different clubs you can drift apart but we've got a group that will be friends forever. As well as playing for a massive club and having really nice memories that's one of the best things that I took from Southampton. Being able to create a friendship with people you truly trust with anything is something I will treasure more than anything.

Kelvin is someone who commands respect and when you speak to him you know you're going to get brutal honesty from him. He doesn't pull any punches and when you ring him for advice or to run things by him you know he'll be as truthful and honest as he possibly could for your benefit. I think he's the type of person that you'd much rather have in your life than not. You can't miss out Kelly either. She is an unbelievable girl who has kept the ship steady while he does his thing on the pitch. They are an outstanding family that we are proud to be friends with. We cherish them and I spent a month at their home and I was part of the family. A really great family and I can't speak highly enough about them.

It's a privilege to call them friends."

....

Here is a message from former team mate and friend **Adam Lallana** who is clearly looking forward to returning to St Mary's for the testimonial match in May:

"Kelvin, well, what can I say mate? A huge congratulations to you and your family on this amazing achievement.

I was lucky enough to experience the majority of your time at Southampton with you. I struggle to remember the baby faced, clean shaven Kelvin Davis that signed for Saints back in 2006.

One of my favourite memories was the promotion from League One and the party we had with the squad in Vegas and Wotto surprising us all at the airport and coming on the trip with us!

I hope you have a great day and I'm looking forward to see so many familiar faces. Enjoy it mate. Adz".

Two people who have been massive influences on Kelvin's career are Malcolm Webster and Keith Granger.

First, let us hear from the person he calls his mentor, goalkeeping coach **Malcolm Webster**, who is still coaching at Ipswich Town.

Malcolm has always tried to instil the work ethic in young goalkeepers. As he says, *"One or two might have rebelled but Kelvin definitely wasn't one of them. Like the majority Kelvin wanted that work ethic, that guidance".* Malcolm has always been a great believer in *"the harder we worked, the easier it became".* He is pleased that all the goalkeepers he has worked with have followed his guidance simply because they recognise *"what it does for them on a Saturday".*

Malcolm knows that Kelvin worked at all aspects of his trade. He points out, *"When he first came to Southampton, he'd always had issues with his kicking. He is such a powerful excellent kicker of the ball that he would have to do extra sessions on his glutes and things like that".* He can remember Kelvin being *"a little bit sceptical about things like Pilates"* but he soon recognised that it could give him longevity in his career.

Malcolm says that, in addition to the morning sessions, they would train in the afternoon albeit these sessions would last just 40 minutes. Kelvin would never grumble and would stay to train.

Malcolm also describes how in the summer he would meet three of four 'keepers, including Richard Wright, at the local park. He feels this revealed a determination and degree of dedication that people might never see. Malcolm stresses what so many others have said and that is that Kelvin was full of dedication. When he came out to train he would be fully committed. During a session a remark might be made that would result in the whole group having to stop and laugh. Kelvin would just carry on but it'd take the others five minutes before they could get started again.

Malcolm recalls a moment when Kelvin was at Luton, *"Anglia television came over to do some filming. I think it was probably for a cup match. He actually caught a ball but instead of looking at the ball he dived smiling at the camera. Even the cameraman couldn't believe it".* Is this perhaps what Alan Pardew saw? The X factor in Kelvin?

Malcolm continues by saying that Kelvin was highly professional, never taking his eye off the ball but at the same time, *"his humour is inbred in him".*

It is clear that Kelvin's sense of humour has served him well in his captaincy roles at Southampton and as Malcolm says, *"I've only ever known him like that. Even when he was young he'd do things that I would cringe at, to say the least. I would cringe at some of the things he'd do or say when he was only a young lad of 17 or 18".* It was difficult to believe sometimes and Malcolm would find himself thinking, *"How could he do that?"*

To illustrate this Malcolm describes how the Luton players used to train at the rugby club in Luton but get changed at Kenilworth Road. *"Kelvin would walk back into Kenilworth Road with mud up to the eyebrows. Covered in it. He would just strip off in the room where the lady would do all the washing. He'd throw his kit on the floor and he'd be stood there just in his boots. She wouldn't even turn round but just say, 'Thank you, Kelvin'. He would have nothing else on – just his boots. He was the only person who could get away with it – none of us could – he used to get away with those sorts of things. I don't think he even did it to shock, he wasn't trying to belittle her but if anyone else had done it I think there would have been uproar. I think they'd have been straight to the secretary of the club and complaining but because it's him nothing was said. That was when he was a young lad and he already had that sense of humour then".*

Malcolm remembers how Kelvin and his young team mate at Luton, Nathan Abbey climbed through the coach's window one night and *"frightened him to death"* – his room was up on the second floor. Malcolm peruses *"Who could get away with that? Only Kelvin. But I don't think anyone could ever take offence to the fella".*

Kelvin knows right from wrong and, consequently, his jokes and pranks are never harmful. For Malcolm it stems from the way he has been brought up and the way he is with his life. He seems to be able to get away with things that others cannot but *"it is not because he's Kelvin Davis the goalkeeper but because he's Kelvin Davis the person".*

Two of Kelvin's qualities that are most frequently cited are respect and loyalty, both of which have to be shared and earned. *"I think that for Kelvin that is a family thing. It comes from Geoff and Lily. The support they've given him over the years is easy in football in the good times when you're playing well, but in the bad times they were there for him and it must have been really difficult for them at times".*

Malcolm continues, *"Take away all the attributes and all the other things and his goalkeeping ability is second to none, his technique is second to none".* Malcolm currently has a goalkeeper at Ipswich, Dean Gerken, who used to train with Kelvin when Dean was at Colchester United at Kelvin was at Ipswich. Malcolm describes how Dean talks about Kelvin even now with real admiration for the way Kelvin worked as a goalkeeper.

Malcolm likes to think that all his goalkeepers have not only the all-important work ethic but that they have a caring attitude for everybody involved in their lives and not just football people. *"I care about people and I don't expect my goalies not to care".* When people talk about him it is crystal clear that such a caring attitude runs through Kelvin's veins.

Malcolm offers an example of how he behaved as a *"young lad with an old head and he always cared for other people".* Matt Taylor, who once scored against him for Portsmouth, was at Luton and Malcolm recalls a remark he made about Matt to Kelvin one day, *"He could be a good player, him".* Kelvin replied very simply, *"He is a good player".*

This reflects well the positive attitude that shines through from Kelvin and Malcolm reflects that, without such a positive outlook *"the Sunderland thing would have easily finished a lot of people off".* Malcolm had been talking to him a lot through the season at Sunderland and at the end of the season he was keen to see him come to the Saints. Malcolm is proud that he had no doubts about Kelvin, *"When he came down to us he was a bit more scarred than I thought. There wasn't one doubt in my mind that we'd made the right choice even when the goal went in against QPR. No doubt came into my mind that we'd got the right person. I knew eventually through the work that we'd done that he would come through".*

Kelvin is both positive and loyal and Malcolm reflects on the loyalty he has always shown. *"I didn't know him at school but I bet he was as loyal to his school friends as he is to his wife, his mum, his dad, everybody. It's a credit to his Mum and Dad. They're the ones that brought him up, they're the ones that did so much with him. I wouldn't say they did it for him, they did it with him. That's the type of people they are".*

Asked about his favourite moments with Kelvin, Malcolm recalls a semi-final play-off when Ipswich played West Ham. A little lad waited at the side of the goal, *"Kelvin, Kelvin can I have your autograph?"* At the end of the warm-up Kelvin jogged over only for the boy to greet him with an outburst of foul-mouthed abuse even with his Dad standing right next to him! It is a favourite recollection for Malcolm because for once Kelvin was *"lost for words".*

Malcolm also recalls another favourite moment which was the "turning point" at Sheffield Wednesday. As described earlier there were a few choice words but Kelvin turned things round. As Malcolm observes with an element of sympathy for players and especially goalkeepers, *"You can't abuse anyone like that anywhere else. You only get it in football grounds".*

When he considers what Kelvin might achieve in the future Malcolm is in good company with other people when he says simply: *"Anything he wants. If he puts his mind to whatever he wants to do he will do it".*

As for a possible future with Southampton Malcolm thinks it all depends on the nature of the role. *"When you talk in football terms you've got the football side itself, you've got the commercial side of it all, then you've got the PR side. I think whatever he does is important to him and he just puts everything into whatever he does".*

If someone came in for him from a lower league Malcolm's advice would be *"Stop where you are".* But if he did choose to go down the leagues he'd be *"the best 'keeper in that league".* Malcolm is honest and expresses his opinion that Kelvin is not yet ready to coach. However, he goes on to offer this appraisal, *"I think he could develop into a very good coach if that's what he chose because that is Kelvin. I think with Kelvin there's more to him than that. I'm not belittling goalkeeping coaches and of course he's got a lot of knowledge and he's gone through the psychology side of it – living proof of it and in retrospect I think the psychology side of Kelvin is as important as the technical, the fitness and the things that go with it – he's come through all that and to be fair he's come through with flying colours".*

With a broad smile Malcolm offers the best summary statement of what Kelvin could achieve in his future, *"If he says he wants to be a bin man he'll be the best bin man in the county. If you didn't put your bin out he'd do it for you because he just cares. He's a caring person. I can't think of anything that he wouldn't be very good at".*

....

Keith Granger now scouts for the FA as well as continuing to coach (his call sign is GKbyKG which is Goalkeeping by Keith Granger) and what he says about Kelvin is full of pride and affection.

Keith had been training the academy goalkeepers but stepped in to help with the first team when needed. He recalls that one day Malcolm pulled him to one side and said, *"We're going to sign a lad and you'll love him".* He found out that the *"lad"* was Kelvin Davis who was coming from the north east off the back of a less than comfortable experience up there. When Kelvin arrived it took Keith days, not weeks, to realise that Malcolm was absolutely right. According to Keith, Kelvin simply *"came across as a nice bloke. You know then that you want to help the guy and help him improve because he has no negativity about him".*

Kelvin's former team mate Richard Wright came to the Saints on loan when Kelvin got injured. Keith claims with a smile that the injury happened when *"he trapped his finger in some shorts when going up for a cross and from then on he played with pockets turned out in training so that it didn't happen again".*

Keith really started working on programmes when *"backs were against the wall".* The club was in crisis and *"without character and without a leader"* survival would be out of reach. But the crisis helped to show what Kelvin *"stood for".* He was quoted on television before one game for saying, *"Make sure everyone gets paid before the players".* As always he displayed pure unselfishness, respecting everyone in and around the club. For Keith, *"It's what makes him different, makes him special".*

Keith says that when he and Kelvin started working together he needed to engage Kelvin so that *"my"* programme became *"our"* programme – Kelvin could see the purpose and the reasons behind what they were doing, and the way they were doing it. Keith sought to raise the standards every day and he set two goals for Kelvin. The first was about making improvement on improvement now in order to offer greater longevity in his career and he completely *"bought into that".*

The shorter-term goal was for Kelvin to work hard and perform so that he attracted Premier League interest. Keith wanted to take his focus away from the club in crisis and for him to realise that he could achieve even if otherwise, things were going against them. With this in mind Keith would *"turn over every stone"* to help to make Kelvin better. As mentioned earlier Keith used DVDs to offer feedback on both training and on performances in games and this helped Kelvin immensely.

Keith states that his style of goalkeeper is a *"front-foot goalkeeper"* who can protect the space in front of him with an ability to come and sweep or clear up as well as repositioning to protect the goal. Kelvin fits the bill.

Keith describes how he did a lot of work on concentration and mental focus with Kelvin in the knowledge that goalkeepers need to be alert particularly when there might be large parts of the game when they are being called on to do nothing. If Kelvin did something special Keith would say *"Get out, I'm having it"* which means that even if there were further repeats planned he could stop because he had reached the required standard.

Kelvin responded well to that and what helped was that he was open to any parts of the programme that Keith devised, even if he did have questions or seek clarification.

As well as working together so closely in training Keith and Kelvin used to go to charity events and they were never afraid to have a laugh and enjoy their evenings.

They went to one such event run by a friend of Keith's. As well as Kelvin another guest was Craig David who was being *"looked after by a big burly security man and Kelvin had me"*. Kelvin was standing right behind the security man so Keith shoved the man in the back who turned and glared at Kelvin thinking he had done it. Keith says, *"It was a funny moment for me but I have to say that Kelvin didn't back down. He stood his ground"*.

Another tale comes from when they were training with other Saints' goalkeepers. There was an open window in the building alongside the training pitch and it housed the computer room. Tongue in cheek Keith challenged them to kick the ball through the open window. To his surprise they accepted the challenge. The first attempts were decent shots but all missed. Keith threw the ball to Kelvin who caught it and half-volleyed what Keith calls the *"most excellent strike you'll ever see. The ball took off like a plane and it would have been perfect if it had been three inches to the right"*. The ball went straight through the window but not the one that was open. The computer room was covered in glass and Alan Fox came down thinking there was a burglary or something similar. Keith made up a story that Kelvin had made a terrific save and the ball had spun up towards the window. Davis got away with it again!

To this day Kelvin calls Keith *"kitty"*. The Dutch manager Jan Poortvliet could never say Keith properly. It was *"Keit"* and then it was *"quiche"* then one day *"kitty"* came out. Kelvin jumped on it along with Paul Wotton and that was it. It's *"kitty"* or *"kitty kat"* and that's how it is.

Keith cannot help comparing Kelvin with three Saints' goalkeepers that he had worked with. First, there is Peter Shilton who was *"unique"* and who *"worked very hard every day"*. Then there is John Burridge who *"maximised everything he had"*. Finally, Tim Flowers who was a natural and an up-and-coming international who was *"full of character"*.

Keith says that the highest compliment he can pay Kelvin is that *"he reminds me of traits from all three"*. He continues, *"He is a top professional, loyal, technically excellent, physically committed and he has got character and personality in abundance. That means that whenever there's a negative or anything like that, he has the ability to bounce back from it. That is a huge part of his make-up as well as his ability in protecting the goal".*

But what is really important is that as well as Kelvin being a true professional Kitty is proud to have him as a good friend.

....

CURRENT PLAYERS AND COLLEAGUES:

Steven Davis: *"He's been great since I came to the club. He's the first port of call when anyone comes into the club. He makes you feel welcome and he's obviously a big character. He's got a lot of influence in the whole dressing room not only by the standards that he sets but he's a great personality.*

He has a good laugh and I think he's got a really good balance in his personality. He's been a big part of the club's success which is to his credit".

José Fonte: *"First of all, it has been a pleasure to share the dressing room with him. He's been an amazing figure, an inspiration, a top professional and how a football player should behave and should act. He has helped us a lot to come up the leagues. He's a tremendous goalkeeper and above all he's a great guy, a great person. Any kid in the academy and growing up should aim to be like Kelvin Davis because he's a great person and a great character in the dressing room.*

He only wants the best and demands the best and I have learned a lot from him in my captaincy now, in the role that he has had along the years. For me it was just a pleasure to share the dressing room and all the memories that we have had together and all the fun - mostly the fun, we didn't have many bad and it's a fantastic pleasure to share so many memories with him. It's difficult to pick one memory because we've had so many – all the promotions. We've been together now six years since 2010.

We've shared so many victories, so many fun moments and it's difficult to say one but I would say the day that we played Brighton away. Brighton had been all year unbeaten and we were being taunted as we walked on the pitch that they were the champions and stuff like that. But we went there and in the last minute he made the assist for me to score the goal. I would say that day was very special for me and for us. I have so many memories of him and it's been a good journey. The funny moment was when I saw the video I saw Kelvin Davis looking at the Brighton bench and making fun of them!"

Emma Gimpel: *"It has been an honour to work with Kelvin. He definitely inspired me to be the practitioner that I am now and to see how what I do can work well when someone is committed. He has been for me an example of how you can get a great outcome from prehab. I class him as a friend and it has been great to work with him and hopefully in the future he won't be going too far.*

His charisma is infectious and he would make me smile, he would make me cringe, he would make me blush and want to cry all in the same conversation with the things he used to come out with. He worked very hard to make me feel embarrassed with his cheekiness around the time when my husband Mo and I were about to get married.

He can come into a room and change the dynamics there within seconds. That's why he's our captain, that's why he remains our captain even though he's not been on the pitch. He is a genuinely nice guy. People like Kelvin are rare, he's a rare breed".

Fraser Forster: *"He's a top professional. He helped me massively when I first came to the club and he couldn't have made me feel any more welcome. I think every kind of player who joins the club would say that about him. He's a really nice guy who helps you every way he can.*

It's an honour to train with him every day and we have a good laugh. He keeps me going and he knows the right time to be serious and to chat to you and he knows the time to have a laugh and take your mind off stuff. For me he's been brilliant, a top, top guy and

I can't really thank him enough for everything he's done for me whilst I've been at the club. We've had some great days and it's been fun".

Sammy Lee: *"Since I've been here he epitomises the football club. From where it was – and everyone knows where it was – to where we are now and it's in no small part down to Kelvin Davis. And that's not overstating the case – far from it.*

His influence is in and around the place, in the dressing room and away from the dressing room and he epitomises the rise, and continued rise of this football club".

Gaston Ramires: *"He's a great person, a good professional. I know him and his career and he has good experience that always helps the team. He has always supported you and so I love this boy".*

Suzanne Scott: *"It has been a privilege to work with Kelvin over the past 10 seasons. His training and performance mentality – 100% effort and 100% focus for 100% of the time - is unique. It's hard to imagine a better role model for professional football or more intelligent ambassador for Saints and what this club has achieved".*

Victor Wanyama: *"I have been here three years and I've never seen such a captain. He's a really good man and he always likes to help and he is always there for the players.*

It's just amazing to have someone like Kelvin in the dressing room. I think he is definitely a motivation and people listen. He has been an absolutely fantastic keeper for Southampton and he has been good for the past years. He has been good for us and the new players. He has been talking to them, making them feel at home.

I've never seen a captain like him in a club. I think he is a fantastic man".

James Ward-Prowse: *"He's one of the most influential characters within the group. Without him my experience in the first team, especially when I was younger, wouldn't* *have been the same. The way he welcomed me through the door. He brought me and some of the others into the men's game, if you like.*

He's helped me and being an experienced player I can always go to him with any questions on or off the pitch and he'll always give me the best advice. He's made the place a fun environment to come in and work".

Maya Yoshida: *"He knows about the club having been here a long time. It's not easy to play for the same club more than ten years in England. He has tried to help other players as much as possible including me, especially recently we had the international breaks outside of the country.*

It's not easy to fit in to English football, the English character, but including him the club is a really welcome thing. I think for the new ones it is very easy to join the club and he is a big part of that.

Obviously he is a funny guy and always I sit down next to him. He always helps others".

Greg Baker (Saints Foundation): *"Kelvin has always been a pleasure to work with, and has expressed genuine interest and admiration for the work that the Saints Foundation does across our local community. He has attended a number of our events, and has met and inspired many of our participants. In addition, we are very proud of Kelvin's role as Patron of the Liver and Pancreatic Cancer R&D Charity, with whom he plays an active role in promoting their hugely valuable work".*

....

FAMILY AND FRIENDS:

Emelia (aged 13): *When my friends first heard about my Dad they thought it was cool me having a Dad as a Saint and they were always asking questions about it, "What's it like?" Apart from that everyone's just normal.*

I knew they were my friends from day one and they didn't know about my Dad. I kept it quiet because I didn't want that to be the reason they were my friends. Then it just came out but they've all stayed my friends because it's me.

I feel proud when I watch him play but for me it's normal. I've grown up with it and he's been at the club since I was three. He's been playing since the day I was born. When he does play well I probably feel more excited than he is. I love it but I do get nervous. Sometimes I say I prefer it Dad when you're sitting there because when you're not on the pitch I don't feel as on edge.

I remember Wembley – that was wicked. To have made it all the way through and the whole day was just amazing.

I'm not sure what he'll do next. He's been through loads of questions with lots of people. As far as I know he's just going to see where it goes at the end. I stay out of it because it confuses me, all that stuff.

When we're at home he's quite funny and I do find myself laughing a lot. People come round and say it's just normal here.

Hi Dad, we're VERY PROUD of you for your testimonial and for this book. Your very proud daughter.

Sonnie (aged 11): *The most exciting thing about my Dad is that it means I'm able to watch all the Saints games. He gets me match tickets. As a goalkeeper I think that he's a true leader and he's not the tallest but he can still make some stunning saves.*

When we're at home I like to play footie in the garden. We probably have a play fight. My Dad usually pins me down and then he tickles me.

At school my mates know my Dad's a Saint and they ask for a lot of things. They think it's quite cool supporting Southampton and their friend is the son of a Saint.

LOVE YOU MATE and good luck for the future.

Mum and Dad (Geoff and Lilian): *THANKS SON. After ten years of you playing football at Southampton Football club, we can also reflect upon our journey.*

Whilst playing for other clubs and since you became a Saint, we have travelled to all corners of England and Wales which has enabled us to visit all but three of the total current football league clubs, making Dad's childhood dream a reality.

The whole family are so proud of you, not just for what you have achieved in football, but also for how you are as a person. Your energy to understand better the history of Southampton FC and acknowledge events associated to this club is acclamation to you alone.

We don't know the future, but we certainly know the past. Thank you so much.

Kelly's Mum and Dad (Pat and Val Greening): *Kelvin has been part of our lives for the past 22 years. We are very proud of our association with him and his family and delighted to have him as part of ours.*

Without doubt THE most important thing in his life is his wife and family. Any decisions he's made about his professional life have been based on what's best for them.

A funny person to be around yet conscientious and hard-working and now, a proud member of the 'SAINTS' family.

Duncan Baker (Financial Adviser and friend): *I have known and worked with Kelvin for thirteen years having first met him when he was with Wimbledon FC. It was clear to me from our first meeting that Kelvin knew what he wanted and where he wanted to be not only with his career but also his personal life. Family is very important to Kelvin and he extends his caring nature to his colleagues within football and is seen as a father figure to younger players at the clubs he has played for during his career, providing guidance in many areas including the importance of financial planning for the future. It has been a pleasure working with Kelvin over the years in a relationship that started as a professional working one which I feel has also become a friendship.*

Francis Benali: *I suppose I'd better be complimentary. No, I can't help but not be complimentary.*

He's a very good friend and someone I've got to know better over recent years but what strikes me with Kelvin is a sharp and a very good sense of humour. A character, as people would say but behind that is a very generous, loyal family man that is a good friend.

As we've seen through his service to Southampton somebody that is dedicated and fights for a cause and is loyal to a team. Those qualities stand out not because of the length of time he's been here. When you meet him as a man, as a person, it's not just what he's done on the football pitch which is what as players you are often judged by. What stands him out as a man is how he conducts himself off the pitch as well and that influence he has on the dressing room, on the squad, on the players.

In recent times, he has not played as much as he would have liked – and that comes to most players unless your career is ended abruptly for whatever reason. I had a taste of this myself through my journey as a player. There is an obvious value of seeing a performance in a game but what value can you put on a Kelvin Davis within the dressing room and on the training ground, day in, day out, on the rest of the squad and the club. For me it's immeasurable, you can't put a price or a value on that.

Mohammad Abu Hilal (surgeon and founder of the LAP R&D charity): *I met Kelvin in 2014 and since then I have had the opportunity and the pleasure to know him more as a friend, as a man and as a generous supporter of a human cause. I was amazed to find in him a huge interest in knowing about medical conditions especially about cancer. When I described to Kelvin how pancreatic cancers can be a truly devastating disease, I could see the emotions in his eyes. He was touched, interested and keen to know more but most importantly he was adamant that he wanted to do something, to help and support this cause.*

Not long after this, Kelvin joined the Liver and Pancreatic Research and Development cancer charity as a committee member. He was enthusiastic from the beginning, getting involved in every meeting and activity. His lovely wife Kelly was also on board and together they have organised and supported many fund raising events. It was also so nice to see his kids at some events.

Despite his busy life Kelvin has always been there, like every other committee member. The LAP R&D cancer charity is run by patients and patients' families and for all of us Kelvin's interest and dedication has been a huge help and a great moral support.

Javier Igeño (Spanish Saints): *I know Kelvin as a great family man and a top person. We all know what his presence has meant to Southampton FC on the pitch. Kelvin has known the ups and downs of this great club. When relegation came, he stepped forward to be a leader and a club man. The influence that Kelvin had in the changing room is well known but it's off the pitch that I have seen Kelvin representing the club with joy and patience.*

I have lots of friends who are Saints fans, living in both Spain and England. When they have travelled to Southampton to see a game, sometimes I have needed help from Kelvin for my guests. He has always really made their day. My mate Dave is to blame for my passion for the Saints since I was 16 and his son Tom was the mascot at the Man City game. I knew Tom would have a great day but I wanted to pay Dave back for his friendship and make sure, through Kelvin, that the day was special. Kelvin spent a lot of time with Tom and the players and the club treated him well. He left with a shirt signed by the team plus another shirt and gloves from Kelvin. Tom's bedroom is now a Saints temple with Kelvin's shirt as the centrepiece on the wall.

Kelvin has done things like this more than once and he knows what the fans mean to the club. But off the pitch in England and Spain I can say that his banter is not so good but it has improved through the years!

Kelvin learned quickly what it means to be a Southampton captain. He is a great goalkeeper and off the pitch he still wears the badge with pride. He is a good friend and a role model as captain. But above all, he is to me, another Francis Benali. He reminds me of Franny off the pitch when he is with the fans and the family. I am glad Kelvin has been part of our club for 10 years, and his family have grown up and settled in Southampton and the whole family has created a big bond with the city.

I cannot mention every moment when I have seen Kelvin cheering someone up, supporting a charity or bringing a big smile from a fan. Kelvin is one of the very few who have been a full-time representative of Saints away from the football. For that he has my respect and he truly deserves his testimonial game. For the time that he has given to my club and its fans, I will come all the way from Spain to Southampton to be with him and his family on such an important day.

Kelvin, MUCHAS GRACIAS POR TODO from Javi.

....

PUNDITS:

Adam Blackmore (Sports Editor, BBC Radio Solent): For me there are two parts to Kelvin as player – the sweeper and the shot-stopper. Over the last decade, whichever division the team has been in, his judgement off his line and his starting position have always been great strengths. It's why he hasn't been sent-off in 10 years at the club, which in the modern game is quite an achievement in itself. Throughout the bad times and the good, he has also been a calm authoritative influence on defenders in front of him and a good communicator, and has been a model professional in the shape he has kept himself in – I think he's smaller and fitter now than he was a decade ago.

I would like to think my relationship with Kelvin has grown in time, and has become more than just a working one. We talk in trust and discuss matches, moments he's had, bad days, good days, and the club through the years. He is a loyal person, we know, but that shows in his desire to see the club succeed as much as he wants to succeed personally. The decision by the club to not extend his playing contract is one that can be debated, but rather than take that and react badly to it, he has shown his maturity by discussing the possibility of other roles within the club, as opposed to playing on elsewhere. That shows how much he values Saints.

He also takes criticism on the chin, and has never reacted to a question I've asked him in a bad way. On one occasion a colleague of mine was talking to him about a clanger he'd made – but thought they were talking to Chris Makin about Kelvin – and even when asked "how do you think Kelvin will react to that mistake?" he just answered it calmly and positively, when he could have had a right go. Such is the measure of the man. That criticism has also come from the stands at times, especially in his first couple of years with the club, but his reaction was always to work harder and get better, not to fall-out of love with the club and move on. Even when he could have gone to West Ham in the administration summer of 2009 and played at a higher level, he stayed and has been at the centre of the club's re-birth. He can also be quite funny, not as funny as he thinks he is, but quite funny!!

When it comes to recalling your memories of him, I'm sure everyone around the club, many fans included, will rightly cite the Leeds United performance at Elland Rd in 2012. But what about the number of morale-boosting crucial penalty saves he's made over the years? An incredible number overall, and his list of victims include some of the best in the game, David Silva, Robin Van Persie, Gareth Barry and many more.

Adam Leitch (Chief Sports Writer, Daily Echo): *Since the day he arrived Kelvin has been a dream to work with. Always personable, friendly and open for a chat, he is one of the last old school players with whom you feel there are no needless barriers. Down the years Kelv has proven his dedication to the club, and one of his greatest qualities has been to always understand instinctively what this club is and the spirit it exudes.*

One of the greatest moments was to see Kelvin winning the Daily Echo Player of the Season award.

Buried deep on my email account are a number of incredibly unfriendly messages I received after sticking up for Kelv in the paper following a couple of errors he made not long after joining Saints.

Kelv himself went through a tough time as a section of the fans gave him some stick. So to see him turn that round in quite astonishing fashion, to become a crowd favourite and even a player of the year, up there with the great names of the past, was just brilliant considering not only is he a fine goalkeeper but a top man too.

Dave Merrington (Sports commentator, BBC Radio Solent): *The first word I would use about Kelvin is outstanding in terms of the influence he has had on the side in all his time at Southampton. I feel that he has often brought composure to the side especially in those days in the lower leagues.*

As a goalkeeper he is one of the best at taking up the right starting position. He is exceptional at marking out his territory and reads the game very well, sometimes acting almost as a 'semi-sweeper'. He is an excellent shot-stopper, always mentally sharp and with terrific awareness and perception as to what is going on around him. I know how much hard work he puts in at training especially with former coach Keith Granger. Keith used to work and work him. I always say that any player must show attitude and Kelvin certainly has this in abundance.

He is not only a super professional but also a super lad. I have always found him very approachable and extremely likeable. Whether in a formal interview or not I have always found Kelvin to be very responsive.

My best memory of him was his display away at Charlton Athletic [in 2008-09] when he made save after save and kept a clean sheet. Some were reaction saves and others at full length. I would give him 10/10 for his performance that day – I normally only ever give 9/10.

In many aspects of life today so-called role models have been decimated and almost disappeared. But I have to say that Kelvin is one of the few remaining role models in the game and I put him in the same category as Alan Shearer and Matt Le Tissier. I really can't speak highly enough of him.

Gordon Simpson (former Daily Echo sports journalist): *I have greatly appreciated the generosity and graciousness with which Kelvin has given his time to me over the years. The responsibility he has shown in speaking during the club's most difficult hours,* *and the eloquence and passion he has displayed in doing so, is something that should not be underestimated. As a result, I have enormous admiration not only for Kelvin Davis as a player, but as a person too.*

....

SAINTS SUPPORTERS:

Liz Aylett (Salisbury):
Loyalty – stayed with us through the bad times.
Leadership – always a strong presence, whether in the team or in the dressing-room.
Likeable – comes across as a really decent person.
Looking good for the future.
In short, one **'L'** of a Saint!

Claire and Jill Brooker (Southampton): *Super Kelvin Davis. The incredible display at Leeds during the Championship promotion year and the late penalty save against Brighton in League One are part of the playing legend. Above all this is Kelvin's club loyalty. To refuse a contract with another club and return to one just out of administration says it all. A true Saint. Thank you.*

Ian Buckle (Southampton): *In these days of mercenary footballers Kelvin deserves credit for his loyalty to the club despite tempting offers elsewhere. Special memories are his spectacular display at Leeds in the Championship and a pre-season friendly at Winchester (might have been Eastleigh). When I asked him after the match who our impressive young centre half was, he replied he didn't have a clue. Hilarious.*

Thanks Kelvin for your great service to our club. Best wishes.

Pete and Sandra Cutler (Salisbury): *Football stars are always idols to their fans, but none more so than those who stick with their clubs through difficult times. Kelvin is a* *perfect example. When Saints were in turmoil Kelvin remained loyal to the club and so he will always be a star to Saints fans. A terrific goalkeeper and a true Saint.*

Mark Fickling (Rownhams): *April Fool's Day 2009 – trading in Saints shares suspended. Not funny. Next day my birthday. Administration. Not funny at all. Ten points deducted and the "Save the Saints" match cancelled due to lack of interest.*

Then we heard the name "Liebherr". Kelvin swerved away from Upton Park. 28 March 2010 and the "Paint Pot" was ours – a happy birthday for me. Then double promotions. Happy again. Thanks Kelvin.

Emma Fitz-Gerald (Southampton): *Super Kel, what can I say? Firstly, thank you for all you've done for the club over the years and for sticking with us through thick and thin. I know you've had positive influence in the dressing room as the other players always seem to talk about your banter in their interviews. I will miss you whipping the other guys on the crossbar challenge on away games and reading your programme notes at home.*

My best memory of you as a player was on a cold night up in Leeds where you put in the most fantastic goalkeeping performance… ever. You kept us in that game and miraculously we earned three points and kept a clean sheet, despite Leeds throwing the kitchen sink at us. Still one of the best one-nil games I've ever seen as a Saints fan. You were a legend that day and will remain a legend in the hearts and minds of all Saints fans.

Thanks for your service to the club and I hope you will look back on your time here fondly and that you will be able to stay involved in the future.

Trudy Hayter (Ferndown): *You have been a superb asset to Southampton Football Club and a great ambassador over the years. We were all so very sad when it looked like your days at the Club had ended but that last minute turnaround makes you even more special to us all.*

Good luck for the future – and may it be forever with the Saints!

Jenny and Claire Hearnden (Southampton): *Professional, reliable, cheeky and mischievous – we could go on. You will be remembered fondly for always playing with a smile on your face. More notably a cheeky grin when trying to kick a ball at your Mum in the crowd and you narrowly missed us.*

Thanks for choosing us over West Ham, our Super Kelv!

Bob Horn (Southampton): *Great servant to the club. Brilliant goalkeeper. Excellent man.*

Ashley Jones (Southampton): *What a fantastic servant, great character and brilliant leader Kelvin Davis has been for Southampton. Will never forget Leeds away and all the times he's saved us. Every club needs a Super Kelvin Davis.*

Amy and Diane Joyce (Southampton): *Thanks Kelvin for all the fantastic games you've been part of through the good and bad times. Hope you'll remain a big part of Southampton Football Club for a very long time. Super Kel. Love to you and your family.*

Patsy Kearns (Salisbury): *Our hero, Kelvin Davis. If anyone doubted his ability all I can say is that perhaps you weren't there in our League One and Championship days especially at away matches when Kelvin single-handedly kept the score down? He was repeatedly named man of the match, especially Leeds away! Who can forget that?*

Thank you, Kelvin for your loyalty.

Nicky and Gavin King (Eastleigh): *We have two overriding memories of Kelvin. The first is how he stayed loyal to us when we were relegated to League One and he turned down the chance to move to West Ham. Secondly, we remember how he single-handedly won the game at Leeds for us, during the Championship promotion season, with a string of amazing saves. As it happens we had to miss that game (a rare occurrence) and watched it on the TV but nevertheless we can still remember it vividly.*

Martyn Last (Littlehampton): *Kelvin Davis has been with the Saints 'forever'. He's stuck with them through thick and thin. He had opportunities to move elsewhere but he stayed with us. He's been a brilliant goalkeeper and he's also been the spirit of Southampton through his leadership.*

Colin and Linda McDougall (Southampton): *We were lucky enough to be on Kelvin's table at the end of season dinner in 2010. He was a fantastic host, happy to answer questions from all the guests and to keep the conversation going. His leadership abilities were clear, with the players all listening to him. We're sure he'll go on to another successful career. Thanks for everything you've given to Saints, Kelvin.*

Keith Mullard (Southampton): *One of my memories is Kelvin making three unbelievable saves in the space of 60 seconds just before half-time at the Valley in November 2008.*

It was a vital relegation battle on a rain soaked pitch. I can still picture the Charlton players shaking their heads at the interval. More good saves followed earning a point in a goalless draw.

Andrew and Anna Murray (Saints Programme Shop): *Congratulations on achieving your 10-year testimonial at Southampton. I've been supporting the Saints now for over 55 years and my favourite players have always been those that have shown loyalty to the club – you are certainly in the category.*

Hopefully when your playing days are over there will still be a role for you to play at St Mary's to continue your positive effect on the club.

Best wishes to you and your family.

Mike Powell (Fleet): *What can you say about Kelv? A fans' favourite who we've named Super Kelv for a reason. A family man who leads by example in every way possible, a true leader and an inspiration to the players of all ages around him. He's never too busy to* *spend time with the fans, or even give us a cheeky wave when we ask him what the score is from behind the goal! It's fair to say that we will never forget Leeds away, a game where Kelv can claim the three points all to himself after a heroic display.*

Thank you for everything you have done for our club through thick and thin, you are a true Saints legend!

Stephen Ridgely (Totton): *Thank you Kelvin for all the fantastic memories and for sticking with us through all the tough times, especially when we were in administration and we had minus ten points in League One. You've been a fantastic servant to the club, one of the best of my generation certainly. I wish you all the best for the future and I hope you remain around the club for many years to come.*

Jordan Sparks (Stubbington): *Kelvin Davis has been an excellent servant to the club. Ten years of service, he stayed with us in the dark days and now here for the good ones. Thank you Kelvin.*

Ken Tollerfield, (Fareham): *When Kelvin signed for Saints back in 2006 I asked a work colleague (a Sunderland supporter) his opinion and he wasn't very complementary and so I was a little concerned about our new keeper. I needn't have worried. Kelvin soon proved his ability as a keeper and his worth to the Saints!*

I consider Kelvin as one of the best shot-stoppers I've ever seen, putting him right up there with Peter Shilton. Kelvin has been very loyal to the Saints and a great ambassador for the club and, importantly, an example for other players to follow.

As the song goes "there's only one Kelvin Davis" and thankfully he's one of us.

Glyn Tudor (Southampton): *When he signed for Saints in 2006, Kelvin had a tough act to follow as the long-term replacement for Antti Niemi. Now 10 years on, although no longer first choice, he is still an important member of the squad. During his time at SMS, he has shown loyalty and consistency and his appointment as club captain reflects* *his standing in the club. Cheerful, modest and a true team player, 'Super Kelv' is a perfect role model for any aspiring young player.*

Alan White (supporter for 60 years, Eastleigh): *… one Kelvin Davis, there's only one Kelvin Davis… stalwart defender of the Saints goal for many years.*

Cameron Whyte (11 years old, Southampton): *An excellent goalie and he's good at saving all the time and keeping us in it. Thank you for helping us.*

Colin and Ruth Young and Rachel Lambden (Reading): *Kelvin, you have been a great servant to the Saints, both on and off the pitch. Your performance at Leeds was probably the best goalkeeping performance we have seen in all our years of watching professional football and key to our promotion to the Premier League. We wish all the best to you and your family on your richly deserved testimonial.*

....

Kelvin acknowledges that so many people have had a huge influence on him both as a player and as a man: players, managers, coaches, medical staff and physiotherapists, club chairmen, directors and all the support staff in football clubs. Not all are mentioned in this book but they are nonetheless held dear by Kelvin.

But there are two groups to whom he will always be highly grateful and a tribute in his captain's notes in the Walsall programme on 7 May 2011 still stands as a testimony to his feelings during his ten seasons as a Saints player:

*"A huge thank you also has to go out to the **wives and girlfriends of the players** who have been so supportive as we have been away for long periods over the last nine months and of course, the last tribute is to **you guys** for your backing and loyalty through the good and bad times over the past couple of years. All the Southampton players appreciate the time and money our supporters put into following us up and down the country".*

It is indisputable that, in both football and in other areas of life, loyalty breeds loyalty. The loyalty of Kelvin Davis to the Saints, including his decision to forego greater riches in order to stay at the club, is why the supporters feel about him the way they do. He chose to stay even when the club appeared to be at an all-time low and he was possibly approaching the peak of his career.

There can be no better way of showing the feelings of supporters, friends and everyone involved with Southampton Football Club than to say simply:

Thanks for staying.

Thanks and Acknowledgements

There are too many people to thank by name for their help in compiling this celebration of Kelvin's ten seasons at SFC.

However, I do want to extend my special thanks to the following:

- Kelly Davis
- Geoff and Lilian Davis
- Pat and Valerie Greening
- Dan Harding
- Ros Wheeler
- Simon Williams
- Leighton Mitchell
- Matt Watson

The following sources have been used:

- www.soccerbase.com
- Southampton FC Match Day programmes and website: saintsfc.co.uk
- All the Saints, David Bull, Gary Chalk, Duncan Holley. Hagiology Publishing, 2013
- The *Herald Express* newspaper (Torquay), Richard Hughes and David Thomas

Photos are courtesy of:

- Southampton Football Club
- The Daily Echo
- The Davis and Greening families

Thanks are also due to the staff of:

- Salisbury Printing
- Bright Yellow Solutions

The Numbers Game

The following shows (season by season) all **301** games in which Kelvin has appeared for the Saints, together with the result of each match.

2006-07	**CHAMPIONSHIP**		**Appearances:**	**44**
06/08/06	DERBY COUNTY	A		DREW 2-2
09/08/06	COVENTRY CITY	H		WON 2-0
12/08/06	WEST BROMWICH ALBION	H		DREW 0-0
19/08/06	BARNSLEY	A		DREW 2-2
23/08/06	YEOVIL TOWN *Carling Cup*	H		WON 5-2
26/08/06	PRESTON	H		DREW 1-1
09/09/06	IPSWICH TOWN	A		LOST 2-1
12/09/06	CRYSTAL PALACE	A		WON 2-0
16/09/06	PLYMOUTH ARGYLE	H		WON 1-0
19/09/06	MILLWALL *Carling Cup*	A		WON 4-0
23/09/06	BURNLEY	A		WON 3-2
30/09/06	QUEENS PARK RANGERS	H		LOST 2-1
14/10/06	LEICESTER CITY	A		LOST 3-2
17/10/06	CARDIFF CITY	A		LOST 1-0
21/10/06	STOKE CITY	H		WON 1-0
24/10/06	NOTTS COUNTY *Carling Cup*	A		LOST 2-0

28/10/06	COLCHESTER UNITED	A	LOST 2-0
01/11/06	WOLVERHAMPTON WANDERERS	H	WON 2-0
04/11/06	HULL CITY	H	DREW 0-0
11/11/06	SUNDERLAND	A	DREW 1-1
18/11/06	LEEDS UNITED	A	WON 3-0
25/11/06	LUTON TOWN	H	WON 2-1
29/11/06	BIRMINGHAM CITY	H	WON 4-3
02/12/06	HULL CITY	A	WON 4-2
09/12/06	SOUTHEND UNITED	A	LOST 2-1
16/12/06	NORWICH CITY	H	WON 2-1
23/12/06	SHEFFIELD WEDNESDAY	A	DREW 3-3
26/12/06	CRYSTAL PALACE	H	DREW 2-2
30/12/06	LEICESTER CITY	H	WON 2-0
01/01/07	PLYMOUTH ARGYLE	A	DREW 1-1
06/01/07	TORQUAY UNITED *FA Cup*	A	WON 2-0
13/01/07	BURNLEY	H	DREW 0-0
20/01/07	QUEENS PARK RANGERS	A	WON 2-0
28/01/07	MANCHESTER CITY *FA Cup*	A	LOST 3-1
31/01/07	SHEFFIELD WEDNESDAY	H	WON 2-1
03/02/07	DERBY COUNTY	H	LOST 1-0
10/02/07	WEST BROMWICH ALBION	A	DREW 1-1

17/02/07	BARNSLEY	H	WON 5-2
20/02/07	COVENTRY CITY	A	LOST 2-1
24/02/07	IPSWICH TOWN	H	WON 1-0
05/03/07	PRESTON	A	LOST 3-1
10/03/07	STOKE CITY	A	LOST 2-1
13/03/07	CARDIFF CITY	H	DREW 2-2
15/05/07	DERBY COUNTY *Championship Play-off*	A	WON 3-2
			Lost on penalties

2007-08	**CHAMPIONSHIP**	**Appearances:**	**38**
18/08/07	NORWICH CITY	A	LOST 2-1
25/08/07	STOKE CITY	H	WON 3-2
01/09/07	QUEENS PARK RANGERS	A	WON 3-0
16/09/07	WATFORD	A	LOST 3-2
19/09/07	COLCHESTER UNITED	H	DREW 1-1
22/09/07	BARNSLEY	H	LOST 3-2
29/09/07	SHEFFIELD UNITED	A	WON 2-1
02/10/07	PRESTON	A	LOST 5-1
06/10/07	WEST BROMWICH ALBION	H	WON 3-2
21/10/07	CARDIFF CITY	H	WON 1-0
24/10/07	BRISTOL CITY	A	LOST 2-1
27/10/07	BURNLEY	A	WON 3-2

03/11/07	CHARLTON ATHLETIC	H	LOST 1-0
06/11/07	WOLVERHAMPTON WANDERERS	H	DREW 0-0
10/11/07	SHEFFIELD WEDNESDAY	A	LOST 5-0
24/11/07	BLACKPOOL	H	WON 1-0
27/11/07	IPSWICH TOWN	A	LOST 2-0
01/12/07	LEICESTER CITY	A	WON 2-1
04/12/07	SHEFFIELD WEDNESDAY	H	DREW 0-0
08/12/07	HULL CITY	H	WON 4-0
15/12/07	COVENTRY CITY	A	DREW 1-1
22/12/07	PRESTON	H	LOST 1-0
26/12/07	COLCHESTER UNITED	A	DREW 1-1
29/12/07	BARNSLEY	A	DREW 2-2
01/01/08	WATFORD	H	LOST 3-0
05/01/08	LEICESTER CITY *FA Cup*	H	WON 2-0
12/01/08	SCUNTHORPE UNITED	H	WON 1-0
19/01/08	PLYMOUTH ARGYLE	A	DREW 1-1
26/01/08	BURY *FA Cup*	H	WON 2-0
29/01/08	NORWICH CITY	H	LOST 1-0
02/02/08	CRYSTAL PALACE	A	DREW 1-1
09/02/08	QUEENS PARK RANGERS	H	LOST 3-2
12/02/08	STOKE CITY	A	LOST 3-2

16/02/08	BRISTOL ROVERS	A	LOST 1-0
19/02/08	PLYMOUTH ARGYLE	H	LOST 2-0
23/0/2/08	SCUNTHORPE UNITED	A	DREW 1-1
01/03/07	IPSWICH TOWN	H	DREW 1-1
04/03/07	WOLVERHAMPTON WANDERERS	A	DREW 2-2

2008-09	**CHAMPIONSHIP**	**Appearances:**	**47**
09/08/08	CARDIFF CITY	A	LOST 2-1
16/08/08	BIRMINGHAM CITY	H	LOST 2-1
23/08/08	DERBY COUNTY	A	WON 1-0
30/08/08	BLACKPOOL	H	LOST 1-0
14/09/08	QUEENS PARK RANGERS	A	LOST 4-1
17/09/08	IPSWICH TOWN	H	DREW 2-2
20/09/08	BARNSLEY	H	DREW 0-0
27/09/08	DONCASTER ROVERS	A	WON 2-0
30/09/08	NORWICH CITY	H	WON 2-0
04/10/08	COVENTRY CITY	A	LOST 4-1
18/10/08	WATFORD	H	LOST 3-0
21/10/08	SHEFFIELD UNITED	A	DREW 0-0
25/10/08	SWANSEA CITY	A	LOST 3-0
28/10/08	COVENTRY CITY	H	DREW 1-1

01/11/08	PRESTON	A	WON 3-2
08/11/08	BRISTOL CITY	H	LOST 1-0
15/11/08	WOLVERHAMPTON WANDERERS	H	LOST 2-1
22/11/08	READING	A	LOST 2-1
25/11/08	PLYMOUTH ARGYLE	H	DREW 0-0
29/11/08	CHARLTON ATHLETIC	A	DREW 0-0
06/12/08	SHEFFIELD WEDNESDAY	H	DREW 1-1
08/12/08	CRYSTAL PALACE	A	LOST 3-0
13/12/08	BURNLEY	A	LOST 3-2
20/12/08	NOTTINGHAM FOREST	H	LOST 2-0
26/12/08	PLYMOUTH ARGYLE	A	LOST 2-0
28/12/08	READING	H	DREW 1-1
04/01/09	MANCHESTER UNITED *FA Cup*	H	LOST 3-0
10/01/09	BARNSLEY	A	WON 1-0
17/01/09	DONCASTER ROVERS	H	LOST 2-1
27/01/09	NORWICH CITY	A	DREW 2-2
31/01/09	SWANSEA CITY	H	DREW 2-2
03/02/09	SHEFFIELD UNITED	H	LOST 2-1
14/02/09	BRISTOL CITY	A	LOST 2-0
21/02/09	PRESTON	H	WON 3-1
28/02/09	CARDIFF CITY	H	WON 1-0

03/03/09	IPSWICH TOWN	A	WON 3-0
07/03/09	BIRMINGHAM CITY	A	LOST 1-0
10/03/09	DERBY COUNTY	H	DREW 1-1
14/03/09	QUEENS PARK RANGERS	H	DREW 0-0
21/03/09	BLACKPOOL	A	DREW 1-1
04/04/09	CHARLTON ATHLETIC	H	LOST 3-2
07/04/09	WATFORD	A	DREW 2-2
10/04/09	WOLVERHAMPTON WANDERERS	A	LOST 3-0
13/04/09	CRYSTAL PALACE	H	WON 1-0
18/04/09	SHEFFIELD WEDNESDAY	A	LOST 2-0
25/04/09	BURNLEY	H	DREW 2-2
03/05/09	NOTTINGHAM FOREST	A	LOST 3-1

2009-10	**LEAGUE ONE**	**Appearances:**	**49**
08/08/09	MILLWALL	H	DREW 1-1
11/08/09	NORTHAMPTOWN TOWN *Carling Cup*	A	WON 2-0
15/08/09	HUDDERSFIED TOWN	A	LOST 2-1
18/08/09	SWINDON TOWN	A	LOST 1-0
22/08/09	BRENTFORD	H	DREW 1-1
25/08/09	BIRMINGHAM CITY *Carling Cup*	H	LOST 2-1
29/08/09	STOCKPORT	A	DREW 1-1

05/09/09	COLCHESTER UNITED	H	DREW 0-0
12/09/09	CHARLTON ATHLETIC	A	DREW 1-1
19/09/09	YEOVIL TOWN	H	WON 2-0
26/09/09	CARLISLE UNITED	A	DREW 1-1
29/09/09	BRISTOL ROVERS	H	LOST 3-2
03/10/09	GILLINGHAM	H	WON 4-1
06/10/09	TORQUAY UNITED (JPT)	H	2-2 (5-3 pens)
09/10/09	SOUTHEND UNITED	A	WON 3-1
17/10/09	OLDHAM ATHLETIC	A	WON 3-1
24/10/09	MK DONS	H	WON 3-1
31/10/09	LEYTON ORIENT	A	DREW 2-2
06/11/09	BRISTOL ROVERS	A	WON 3-2
15/11/09	BRIGHTON AND HOVE ALBION	H	LOST 3-1
21/11/09	NORWICH CITY	H	DREW 2-2
24/11/09	HARTLEPOOL UNITED	A	WON 3-1
02/01/10	LUTON TOWN *FA Cup*	H	WON 1-0
16/01/10	MILLWALL	A	DREW 1-1
20/01/10	MK DONS (JPT)	A	WON 1-0
23/01/10	IPSWICH TOWN *FA Cup*	H	WON 2-1
26/01/10	BRENTFORD	A	DREW 1-1
30/01/10	STOCKPORT	H	WON 2-0

06/02/10	EXETER CITY	A	DREW 1-1
09/02/10	MK DONS	H	WON 3-1
13/02/10	PORTSMOUTH *FA Cup*	H	LOST 4-1
20/02/10	NORWICH CITY	A	WON 2-0
23/02/10	WYCOMBE WANDERERS	A	DREW 0-0
27/02/10	WALSALL	H	WON 5-1
02/03/10	HUDDERSFIELD TOWN	H	WON 5-0
06/03/10	TRANMERE ROVERS	A	LOST 2-1
13/03/10	LEEDS UNITED	H	WON 1-0
16/03/10	SWINDON TOWN	H	LOST 1-0
20/03/10	MK DONS	A	WON 3-0
23/03/10	HARTLEPOOL UNITED	H	WON 3-2
28/03/10	CARLISLE UNITED *JPT Final at Wembley Stadium*		WON 4-1
01/04/10	BRIGHTON AND HOVE ALBION	A	DREW 2-2
05/04/10	LEYTON ORIENT	H	WON 2-1
10/04/10	CHARLTON ATHLETIC	H	WON 1-0
13/04/10	BRISTOL ROVERS	A	WON 5-1
17/04/10	YEOVIL TOWN	A	WON 1-0
20/04/10	OLDHAM ATHLETIC	H	DREW 0-0
24/04/10	CARLISLE UNITED	H	WON 3-2

| 01/05/10 | GILLINGHAM | A | LOST 2-1 |
| 08/05/10 | SOUTHEND UNITED | H | WON 3-1 |

| **2010-11** | **LEAGUE ONE** | | **Appearances:** | **50** |

07/08/10	PLYMOUTH ARGYLE	H	LOST 1-0
10/08/10	BOURNEMOUTH LEAGUE CUP	H	WON 2-0
21/08/10	LEYTON ORIENT	H	DREW 1-1
24/08/10	BOLTON WANDERERS	H	LOST 1-0
28/08/10	BRISTOL ROVERS	A	WON 4-0
31/08/10	SWINDON TOWN JPT	H	LOST 3-0
04/09/10	ROCHDALE	H	LOST 2-0
11/09/10	SWINDON TOWN	A	LOST 1-0
15/09/10	MK DONS	A	LOST 2-0
18/09/10	COLCHESTER UNITED	H	DREW 0-0
25/09/10	SHEFFIELD WEDNESDAY	A	WON 1-0
28/09/10	YEOVIL TOWN	A	DREW 1-1
02/10/10	BOURNEMOUTH	H	WON 2-0
09/10/10	TRANMERE ROVERS	H	WON 2-0
16/10/10	HUDDERSFIED TOWN	A	LOST 2-0
23/10/10	OLDHAM ATHLETIC	H	WON 2-1
30/10/10	NOTTS COUNTY	A	WON 3-1

02/11/10	DAGENHAM & REDBRIDGE	H	WON 4-0
06/11/10	SHREWSBURY TOWN FAC	H	WON 2-0
13/11/10	CARLISLE UNITED	A	LOST 3-2
20/11/10	PETERBOROUGH UNITED	H	WON 4-1
23/11/10	BRIGHTON & HOVE ALBION	H	DREW 0-0
11/12/10	BRENTFORD	H	LOST 2-0
28/12/10	HUDDERSFIELD TOWN	H	WON 4-1
01/01/11	EXETER CITY	H	WON 4-0
03/01/11	DAGENHAM & REDBRIDGE	A	WON 3-1
11/01/11	OLDHAM ATHLETIC	A	WON 6-0
15/01/11	NOTTS COUNTY	H	DREW 0-0
22/01/11	TRANMERE ROVERS	A	LOST 2-0
01/02/11	EXETER CITY	A	WON 2-1
05/02/11	PETERBOROUGH UNITED	A	DREW 4-4
12/02/11	CARLISLE UNITED	H	WON 1-0
22/02/11	HARTLEPOOL UNITED	A	DREW 0-0
26/02/11	SWINDON TOWN	H	WON 4-1
01/03/11	WALSALL	A	LOST 1-0
05/03/11	COLCHESTER UNITED	A	WON 2-0
08/03/11	YEOVIL TOWN	H	WON 3-0

12/03/11	BOURNEMOUTH	A	WON 3-1
19/03/11	SHEFFIELD WEDNESDAY	H	WON 2-0
22/03/11	CHARLTON ATHLETIC	A	DREW 1-1
02/04/11	MK DONS	H	WON 3-2
05/04/11	CHARLTON ATHLETIC	H	WON 2-0
09/04/11	LEYTON ORIENT	A	WON 2-0
12/04/11	ROCHDALE	A	LOST 2-0
16/04/11	BRISTOL ROVERS	H	WON 1-0
23/04/11	BRIGHTON & HOVE ALBION	A	WON 2-1
25/04/11	HARTLEPOOL UNITED	H	WON 2-0
30/04/11	BRENTFORD	A	WON 3-0
02/05/11	PLYMOUTH ARGYLE	A	WON 3-1
07/05/11	WALSALL	H	WON 3-1

2011-12	**CHAMPIONSHIP**	**Appearances:**	**45**
06/08/11	LEEDS UNITED	H	WON 3-1
13/08/11	BARNSLEY	A	WON 1-0
16/08/11	IPSWICH TOWN	A	WON 5-2
20/08/11	MILLWALL	H	WON 1-0
27/08/11	LEICESTER CITY	A	LOST 3-2
10/09/11	NOTTINGHAM FOREST	H	WON 3-2

18/09/11	BIRMINGHAM CITY	H	WON 4-1
24/09/11	BURNLEY	A	DREW 1-1
28/09/11	CARDIFF CITY	A	LOST 2-1
01/10/11	WATFORD	H	WON 4-0
15/10/11	DERBY COUNTY	A	DREW 1-1
18/10/11	WEST HAM UNITED	H	WON 1-0
22/10/11	READING	A	DREW 1-1
29/10/11	MIDDLESBROUGH	H	WON 3-0
01/11/11	PETERBOROUGH UNITED	H	WON 2-1
05/11/11	COVENTRY CITY	A	WON 4-2
19/11/11	BRIGHTON & HOVE ALBION	H	WON 3-0
26/11/11	BRISTOL CITY	A	LOST 2-0
29/11/11	HULL CITY	H	WON 2-1
03/12/11	DONCASTER ROVERS	A	LOST 1-0
18/12/11	PORTSMOUTH	A	DREW 1-1
26/12/11	CRYSTAL PALACE	H	WON 2-0
30/12/11	BRISTOL CITY	H	LOST 1-0
02/01/12	BRIGHTON & HOVE ALBION	A	LOST 3-0
14/01/12	NOTTINGHAM FOREST	A	WON 3-0
23/01/12	LEICESTER CITY	H	LOST 2-0

31/01/12	CARDIFF CITY	H	DREW 1-1
04/02/12	BIRMINGHAM CITY	A	DREW 0-0
11/02/12	BURNLEY	H	WON 2-0
14/02/12	WEST HAM	A	DREW 1-1
18/02/12	DERBY COUNTY	H	WON 4-0
25/02/12	WATFORD	A	WON 3-0
03/03/12	LEEDS UNITED	A	WON 1-0
06/03/12	IPSWICH TOWN	H	DREW 1-1
10/03/12	BARNSLEY	H	WON 2-0
17/03/12	MILLWALL	A	WON 3-2
20/03/12	HULL CITY	A	WON 2-0
24/03/12	DONCASTER ROVERS	H	WON 2-0
31/02/13	BLACKPOOL	A	LOST 3-0
07/04/12	PORTSMOUTH	H	DREW 2-2
09/04/12	CRYSTAL PALACE	A	WON 2-0
13/04/12	READING	H	LOST 3-1
17/04/12	PETERBOROUGH UNITED	A	WON 3-0
21/04/12	MIDDLESBROUGH	A	LOST 2-1
28/04/12	COVENTRY CITY	H	WON 4-0

2012-13	**PREMIER LEAGUE**		**Appearances:**	**11**
19/08/12	MANCHESTER CITY	A		LOST 3-2
25/08/12	WIGAN ATHLETIC	H		LOST 2-0
02/09/12	MANCHESTER UNITED	H		LOST 3-2
15/09/12	ARSENAL	A		LOST 6-1
30/10/12	LEEDS UNITED LEAGUE CUP	A		LOST 3-0
08/12/12	READING	H		WON 1-0
22/12/12	SUNDERLAND	H		LOST 1-0
26/12/12	FULHAM	A		DREW 1-1
29/12/12	STOKE CITY	A		DREW 3-3
30/03/13	CHELSEA	H		WON 2-1
19/05/13	STOKE CITY	H		DREW 1-1
2013-14	**PREMIER LEAGUE**		**Appearances:**	**8**
27/08/13	BARNSLEY LEAGUE CUP	A		WON 5-1
24/09/13	BRISTOL CITY LEAGUE CUP	H		WON 2-0
06/11/13	SUNDERLAND LEAGUE CUP	A		LOST 2-1
29/12/13	EVERTON	A		LOST 2-1
01/01/14	CHELSEA	H		LOST 3-0
04/01/14	BURNLEY FA CUP	H		WON 4-3
25/01/14	YEOVIL TOWN FA CUP	H		WON 2-0
15/02/14	SUNDERLAND FA CUP	A		LOST 1-0

2014-15	**PREMIER LEAGUE**		Appearances:	**7**
21/03/15	BURNLEY	H		WON 2-0
04/04/15	EVERTON	A		LOST 1-0
11/04/15	HULL CITY	H		WON 2-0
18/04/15	STOKE CITY	A		LOST 2-1
25/04/15	TOTTENHAM HOTSPUR	H		DREW 2-2
02/05/15	SUNDERLAND	A		LOST 2-1
24/05/15	MANCHESTER CITY	A		LOST 2-0
2015-16	**PREMIER LEAGUE**			
17/10/15	LEICESTER CITY	H		DREW 2-2